Invisible Sisters

Invisible Sisters

a memoir

∙∙∙

Jessica Handler

PUBLICAFFAIRS
New York

Published in the United States by PublicAffairs™, a member of the
Perseus Books Group.

Printed in the United States of America.

To protect their privacy, the names and in some cases identifying details of most individuals other than members of my immediate family have been changed.

Portions of this book have appeared in different form in *Ars Medica*; *Brain, Child: The Magazine for Thinking Mothers*; *The Healing Muse*; *The Pebble Lake Review*; and *storySouth*.

PublicAffairs books are available at special discounts for bulk purchases in the U.S. by corporations, institutions, and other organizations. For more information, please contact the Special Markets Department at the Perseus Books Group, 2300 Chestnut Street, Suite 200, Philadelphia, PA 19103, call (800) 810-4145, ext. 5000, or e-mail special.markets@perseusbooks.com.

Designed by Jeff Williams
Text set in 11.5-point New Caledonia by the Perseus Books Group

Library of Congress Cataloging-in-Publication Data
   Handler, Jessica.
   Invisible sisters : a memoir / Jessica Handler.—1st ed.
     p. cm.
   ISBN 978-1-58648-648-8 (hardcover : alk. paper)
   1. Handler, Jessica. 2. Sisters—United States—Biography. 3. Sisters—United States—Death—Psychological aspects. 4. Bereavement—United States—Psychological aspects. I. Title.

BF723.S43H33 2009
155.9'37092—dc22
[B]

                                          2008051489

First Edition

10 9 8 7 6 5 4 3 2 1

For My Family, Before and After.

Acknowledgments

My thanks to Gabriella Burman, Elizabeth Dulemba, Jilly Dybka, Erika Goldman, Rachel Hanson, Beth Lilly, Tom Lombardo, Sherry McHenry, Sandra Novack, and Dr. Gabriel Zatlin for their valuable comments on early drafts. Thank you to the wonderful directors and faculty of Queens University of Charlotte's MFA program for cultivating such an inspiring environment for writers. So much gratitude goes to my agent, Sorche Fairbank, for her powers of perception and her unfailing belief in my work, and to the talented editor Morgen Van Vorst, for getting to the heart of it, time after time. Thank you to my friends at PublicAffairs, who believe in what matters.

This book never would have happened without my mother, Miriam Handler, who gave tangibles and intangibles in her willingness to go spelunking, and to Mickey, without whom I can make no journey large or small.

Making the Dream Life

I daydream about my sisters all the time. One whispers in my ear as I write; another suggests an afternoon snack. Look, an old round Volvo, I say aloud to no one when changing lanes on the freeway. We were sentimental about those tanklike little cars. Our parents each had one when we were small, a green one for Mom, a red one for Dad. The license plate numbers even matched, different by a single digit.

When the weather is warm, I daydream about an imaginary afternoon on a late summer vacation, the three of us together. Susie and Sarah and I lie on the periphery of a body of water, a glittering blue swimming pool somewhere almost shabby, maybe a motel with microwaves and concrete patios along the Gulf Coast of Florida, or somewhere more beautiful—a salt-sticky beach on Cape Cod. At least one of us makes good money if we have decided to go to the Cape. Mindful of the demands on husbands and kids, we have pried one week from our separate calendars, drawing red-pencil squares around that block of days set aside for soggy towels and frayed tennis shoes that leak sand like cracked hourglasses.

Each of us has had our share of bad love affairs, dropped out of school, gone back to school. We have traveled to Europe or out West, slung hash. Gotten speeding tickets. Gotten high. We have gotten married. We have children.

Susie and Sarah and I are devoted to one another, even though we have made our homes in distant cities. Sarah might have studied art history or become a doctor. Or a writer. She was surgically exact with words. Susie, who when she was six wanted to be a nurse, may have earned her doctorate in nursing. If she teaches, her students adore her. She is tough on them, but her laugh is a happy spike in a steady current of energy.

I have not grown up to be the TV star I planned to be when I was eight, flipping my hair and practicing "That Girl's" intoxicating smile. Illya Kuryakin, the Russian secret agent from "The Man from U.N.C.L.E.," did not elope with me. Instead, I am the sister grown up.

My sisters and I have created a tribe of children still unaware that their job will be to remember us. Our sons and daughters see us as moms and indistinctly as sisters; we bicker, and roll our eyes. Keeping peace, we do not speak about certain things: a borrowed car that came back with a cigarette burn in the upholstery, or an emergency loan for a college weekend still unpaid. We snort at Susie's history of boyfriends, Sarah's orderly cooking, my tall tales. We worry about our parents growing old, avoid talking about what we will do when they cannot live alone.

Our dream children look like their mothers. Mine tend toward plumpness, Susie's are forceful and athletic, Sarah's elegant. They shout and argue and make peace in predictable cycles. They smell like the vapor from their sunscreen: baked chemical coconut desserts.

We three lie flat on our backs on chaise longues, near enough to our offspring to stay alert to their safety. "Marco!" my children yell. "Polo!" their cousins holler back. Our husbands never materialize in this fantasy; it is just us.

We sisters drowse in the sun, happy to be side by side with next to nothing to do. As I write this, I am forty-seven, the eldest. Susie would be almost forty-six. Sarah would be forty-two.

part one

∴

Susie, Jessica, Sarah

I.

Sarah died . . . I want to stand in the middle of the room and scream and scream. I can't. I don't know how.

—Journal, 1992

"Are you sitting down?" my mother asked across the long-distance line. We talked on the phone at least once a week, and when I heard her voice, I expected the usual: a "who-can-top-this" tale of her irritating boss, and a sympathetic ear to listen to the latest about my supervisor. Wedging the phone against my shoulder, I walked from the kitchen back to the bedroom, where I had been reading.

Are you sitting down are you sitting down are you sitting down. She was not asking—she was stalling for time. Her voice sounded sped up and wobbly. I knew she was fidgeting, twisting the ring with the three square diamonds on her right forefinger, then spreading her hands wide, flexing them.

I did what my mother asked. I sat down, and kept moving forward, sliding to my knees, and finally crouching on the floor, trying to be so small that the words I knew my mother was going to say would fly above my head. I felt primitive, the way a dog must feel when she hides her head under a rug during a thunderstorm. If no one could see me, I would never have to hear what was coming.

Sarah had prepared me for this day years before. We talked about her death only once, and only then because she forced me. Sarah took the role she often did, that of the big sister, while I acted like the younger woman: blithe, cheerful, and wrongheaded. After a lifetime of surgeries and lab tests, she was preparing for the possibility of a bone marrow transplant, another experiment in a succession of experiments.

Sarah had called me on a weekend afternoon. She lived near our mother outside Boston. I had moved back to Atlanta, where we had grown up.

"This is going to be harder on you than it will be on me," Sarah said.

"I know," I replied.

I was sulky, hating the fact that she had taken control and made me face the truth. While we talked, I imagined Sarah standing in her kitchen, looking out over Dorchester's rooftops and cutting vegetables for a snack she invented when she was a child: raw broccoli stalks dipped in olive oil and salt. Trees, we called them.

"I can handle a hospital stay," I said.

Out of habit, protecting myself, I had dismissed her again. A bone marrow transplant was all this conversation was about. I imagined months in sterile isolation for her, and months for me if I passed the tests to be her donor.

"That's not what I'm talking about," Sarah said. She sounded irritable and urgent. "When I die—that's what I mean."

I made comforting noises, demurring. You won't die from this, don't be silly, this will work, this time will save your life.

"When I die," Sarah said, suddenly fierce, "you will be the only one left."

Crouching on my bedroom floor, my head between my knees and the telephone receiver pushed against my right ear, my mother gave me the news I had dreaded most of my life. Sarah had died.

My mother had lost two daughters, but I had lost all my sisters. Peeled back to its smallest core, my family was now three people: an estranged father, a mother, and me, their first daughter. My sisters were my history, and I was theirs.

Because I wanted to hear Sarah's voice again, I said her words aloud. My voice ricocheted from wall to wall in my quiet house.

"I am the only one left."

2.

A "mutation" can be defined as any change in the primary nucleotide sequence of DNA, regardless of its functional consequences. Some mutations may be lethal, others are less deleterious and in some way may confer an evolutionary advantage.

—Harrison's *Principles of Internal Medicine*, 15th edition

The specific circumstances of medical events that happened to my family may never have happened before. They may never happen again. My sisters suffered illnesses that probably have never been seen in one generation in two siblings at the same time. Because of the kind of leukemia Susie had, our experience was, as one doctor put it, a bizarre coincidence—one that mystified every physician and lab tech we met.

Susie and I shared a big bedroom when we were little, our matching single beds on either side of a window that faced the front yard's ivy-covered slope and pine trees. She fit into my clothes before I was through with them: black velvet jumpers for special occasions, collared blouses, hairy plaid skirts, and cotton pants. Our socks, headbands, and toys were interchangeable; we didn't see any reason we shouldn't be almost the same. Because I was the oldest, Susie expected me to be worldly-wise.

Brushing our teeth side by side at the bathroom sink, Susie stood on a stool at the front, and I leaned in beside her. My job was to know the reason for everything, and I took the responsibility seriously.

"Elephant bells," I explained, "are called that because they are big enough to cover an elephant's feet." We had been admiring the fashionable pants an actress wore on a television variety show, fabric pooling at the hem and obscuring her shoes. Susie, at four or five, had been stymied by naming pants anything other than "pants," but at seven or so, I knew the ways of adults and their clothing.

Our baby sister, Sarah, who was six years younger than I, had her own bedroom across the hall. Susie and I held our fingers out for her to hold while she learned to walk. We were three cherished girls. Our father's father had named his sailboat first for me, then rechristened her twice more, once for Susie, once again for Sarah, finally calling her the *JessSueSar.*

Our mother came to fetch me after midnight when I telephoned her, sobbing, homesick, and eight years old, from my first sleepover. Our father stretched out on his side across the foot of my bed after he tucked me in. Propped up on one elbow, he told me adventure stories about a French unicorn named Charlemagne. Ten years would pass before I learned that Charlemagne had been a medieval king.

Susie pestered our mother at a delicatessen meat department. "Mom, please," she pleaded, shifting from foot to foot.

Pushing her nose against the curved glass case, she couldn't take her gaze away from the scaly, disembodied, gray-clawed chicken feet on ice. Mom gave in and bought a pair, chicken feet that she said the elderly Jewish women in the neighborhood bought to simmer in soup. Susie held her hand up for the white paper package. At kindergarten the following day, she used the splayed yellow feet as stamps in a dish of tempera paint. The other kids pressed hard on raw potato halves to imprint their flower shapes and smiles and trapezoids, but on Susie's strip of brown paper, ghost chickens marched across a paper road.

Several years later, Sarah and her best friend, a boy with hair the red-gold of tiger lilies, set out to earn pocket money from the neighbors with an after-school business. Dog walking, weed pulling, babysitting, whatever needed doing. "Prices Up To YOU!" they wrote on their flyer, adding, "We prefer to work together" in their careful second-grade lettering. Most of their business seemed to come from their own homes, assignment of the simplest tasks conjured by parents and grandparents.

. • .

Every human being has tens of thousands of genes: twenty thousand or more. Genes reside on chromosomes, impossibly tiny threads of DNA strung like beads with the secrets of our future. Most of us have twenty-three pairs of chromosomes orbiting deep in our marrow. How our genes and our chromosomes fall together is the first stroke toward defining who we will be. Our bodies put cells in order within hours of conception. Tall or short, boy or girl, partial to cilantro or likening its taste to soap. Musical or tone deaf, sick or well.

When a cell divides, two identical new cells are made. These are called daughter cells. When they divide again, you have two more daughter cells. Errors can occur. All the genes from the original cell may not make it into the daughter cell. Sometimes more than one copy of a chromosome develops in a daughter cell, diverting normal development. Knowing no history of disease in their past other than the anecdotal—my mother's father was diabetic, a great-aunt on my father's side may or may not have had breast cancer—my parents had little to fear when they decided to have children.

My sister Susie developed leukemia when she was six. My mother said later that Susie's illness seemed to fall from the clear blue sky. Susie was eight when she died, and I was ten. Sarah was four, and had been alternating periods of sickness and health since her birth.

When Sarah was three months old, she was strangely ill, plagued with skin infections that medication couldn't control. After many months of seeking an answer from a phalanx of doctors, someone made the accurate diagnosis of Kostmann's Syndrome. Sarah had an alarmingly low number of granulocytes in her bloodstream, a type of white blood cell key to fighting infection. Her body could manufacture the cells, but they died before they matured.

More than three thousand new cases of acute lymphocytic leukemia—the most common type for children—are diagnosed annually in the United States. The odds of being born with Kostmann's have been described as close to one in two million.

Leukemia and Kostmann's Syndrome are both bone marrow disorders. Leukemia is an abnormal overproduction of white blood cells, Kostmann's Syndrome a deep deficit of the kind that fight infection directly. (Kostmann's Syndrome is variably called agranulocytosis or sometimes called severe congenital neutropenia.)

Lack of white blood cells can be a side effect of chemotherapy, like that used to treat leukemia. Being born without these cells makes for a genetic anomaly. Both parents have to carry the rare gene for Kostmann's Syndrome in order for the disease to be present in their child, and even then, the chances are slim. Kostmann's is not known to be a disorder unique to a particular ethnicity or race, the way that Tay-Sachs disease runs in Ashkenazi Jewish families or sickle-cell anemia among African Americans. Although acute lymphocytic leukemia is not considered a hereditary disease, it can result from changes in genetic structure within the bone marrow. This shift can result from environmental factors or can occur without apparent cause.

The symptoms of Kostmann's Syndrome read like the Passover recitation of the plagues. Instead of the ten ancient plagues that convinced Pharaoh to free the Jews from slavery, more than twenty indicators crowd a list in a medical textbook. Boils and pneumonia gallop out of the gate, with plenty on their heels. Otitis media (ear infections), peritonitis (an infected abdominal wall), gingivitis (gum infections), urinary tract infections.

Leukemia's symptoms are less obscure but are no less frightening. Bruising, fatigue, nosebleeds. Bleeding gums. Headaches. Irritability. Maladies like these can mean any number of things, until someone adds them up.

Pill bottles overflowed our bathroom cabinet when I was young. At eight or nine years old, if I let myself think about it, the mystery unseen in the body could overwhelm me. A trait emerged in me then that ebbed and flowed in me for years: the suspicion that any common symptom hinted at a greater disease. While I sneezed and rubbed my eyes from springtime allergies, I wondered if my sinus headache was really the whisper of a gruesome and fatal tumor, but I kept my fears to myself. I knew worry wouldn't save me.

I had my share of childhood illnesses like everyone else: earaches, seasonal flus, and skinned knees with scabs that wanted picking. When I had chicken pox, we were a normal family with normal childhood illnesses. I have free-floating images of footie pajamas, of chicken-and-stars soup, of playing Chinese checkers with my mother and balancing the metal game board on my blanketed lap.

My sisters' illnesses were extreme. In deference, I bowed out. If being sick in our family made you prominent, then not having a "real" illness, just a runny nose or a fractured wrist from a fall at a roller skating party, began, in my childhood estimation, to erase my place in an imaginary family portrait. I took it as my due. My illnesses did not matter, because they could not.

When I was about nine, the question of mercury weighed heavily on me. Inside the thermometer was a metal that moved, a solid that was liquid. When the thermometer wasn't under Susie's tongue, Mom kept it at the ready, soaking in a juice tumbler of rubbing alcohol.

The thermometer tantalized me. I ordered myself not to reach out and snap the thermometer in half. Instead, I made a habit of slamming the medicine chest shut, enjoying the sound of metal door scraping on metal sill. The day the glass and alcohol and thermometer finally fell from the shelf and broke into pieces in the sink, I was uneasy with my luck. With my forefinger, I pushed the glass shards up the walls of the bowl and out of the way before I prodded a pristine bead of mercury onto my palm. My skin didn't redden or itch as I rolled the tiny ball of fluid along the creases in my hand. I knew not to taste it, but for a few minutes, I was enraptured by the lifelike liquid in my palm.

As I rolled the mercury along my palm, I wondered what danger lurked inside me. When will my turn come? Alarmed, I shook the mercury from my skin, scrubbed my hands red, and cleaned the splintered glass from the sink.

From the outside, you couldn't tell that ours was a family with genetic mutations. I am tall. I am big-boned and have dark hair. I look like what I am: a genetic combination of my parents. Had Susie lived longer than the age of eight, she would have been a tallish woman like me. Her hair was brown and wavy, like mine. In photographs of the two of us together, I see now that her grin was wider than mine, a characteristic of personality rather than genes. Each of us inherited our father's strong jaw, our mother's long limbs. As an adult, Sarah was just five feet tall. She was honey-blonde, her hair color a reach back across many generations. No one in our family is fair, but the original cases of Kostmann's Syndrome, named for the doctor who first identified the illness less than a decade before Sarah's birth, were found in Sweden. Most Swedes are blonde. Sweden is proximate to Russia, Poland, and Lithuania, where my grandparents, their parents, and generations rolling back in time were born. Genes have long memories.

3.

MISS SPANKING-NEW HANDLER . . . WELCOME AND MY
BLESSINGS. YOUR GREAT GREAT GRANDMOTHER ELIZABETH.

—Western Union Telegram,
September 28, 1959, 9:13 PM

My parents were married in the chapel at Brandeis University in Waltham, Massachusetts, on Monday, June 11, 1956. Because theirs was a Jewish wedding, the ceremony couldn't take place on Saturday, the Jewish Sabbath. Sunday was graduation.

That particular June afternoon in Boston was sunny and warm. From photographs, I can conjure the clouds high and slow moving in a sky as blue as morning glories. I look at the black-and-white stiff-backed photos and imagine the frozen images in motion. My parents' families and friends smiled and pecked cheeks thinly coated with perspiration. Men's summer suit jackets were suffocating in the heat.

Women wore white gloves that came just to their wrists and flat hats like flying saucers. On the concrete apron outside the chapel, people smoked. When they were finished, women reapplied crimson lipstick, making kissing shapes into compact mirrors. Men cleared their throats and straightened their ties.

My parents, Mimi and Jack, wore tailored clothes with tight waists. My mother wore a girdle under her wedding dress even though she weighed just over one hundred pounds. At twenty-two, she looked more like sixteen. My parents' dreams, like their clothing, were formal and expected. She would marry, and he would provide.

The Berlin Chapel at Brandeis was pale brick and soaring glass. Just inside the door, a small crowd of guests shuffled like penguins into the sanctuary. My great-grandmother Pauline, who in 1935 had divorced her husband of a Romanian arranged marriage, wore a starburst corsage on her jacket and an extravagant silver bracelet on her wrist. She stood beside her mother, my great-great-grandmother Elizabeth, who was by then stooped like a sea horse. The cord from Elizabeth's hearing aid hung like a leash from her left ear to a chrome battery pack snug in the belt of her dress.

My mother waited at the back of this slow line into the chapel, behind her smiling parents. She held white orchids and carnations. Muted by her veil and backlit by the sun, she looked like a ghost.

After my father kissed his bride, the party repaired to the roof garden at Boston's Hotel Vendome for the reception, after which my parents would change into their "traveling clothes" and leave for a week in Bermuda, reservations made by my father's father.

My parents met when they were freshmen in college, and recognized themselves in each other right away. They looked enough alike to be siblings, dark haired and olive skinned, elegant, and full of life. They were enchanted by how much they had in common; they had both grown up in nonpracticing Jewish families, they loved Thelonius Monk and Dave Brubeck, Dylan Thomas and Emily Dickinson.

My father, Jack, rescued my mother, Mimi, nightly from what he considered an overdose of studying, persuading her to leave the university library to go out for pizza and beer. She always studied in the same spot—a bench by a casement window—so that he could find her. My mother had little experience dating before college, and my father was a magnetic, good-looking man with a promising future, in an era when young women were expected to marry, raise a family, and stay home.

My father honed his glamor in letters to my mother written during summer vacations. Some are twenty pages long and recount parties complete with long lists of friends in attendance, of fishing trips in the mountains and plans for city weekends in New York, halfway between his parents' home in Harrisburg, Pennsylvania, and hers in suburban Boston. Take the four-thirty train, he advised, not the six o'-clock, and he would meet her in the city for dinner. She would stay at his aunt's in Brooklyn Heights, he at a cousin's a block away. Six months younger than Mimi, Jack called her "child," and wrote that love "puts the fright into me."

He praised what he called her perfect delicateness, and conceded to a formal wedding against his will, admitting in a letter, "I do understand how important this wedding is to your parents and I understand that it is right for them to feel as they do. It's their pleasure to be as schmaltzy as they want. I stand to lose nothing (only half a day's inconvenience—but look, I get you)."

In photos of their wedding reception, my father pressed his lips together, folded inward and tense. Mom smiles hugely, and tilts her chin up to accept a kiss. Her brother, who wasn't yet sixteen, clowns behind the wedding cake for the photographer. Pauline, who brooked no nonsense, is captured in that photograph getting to her feet. She looks ready to smack him, probably warning him to sit down already and act his age.

Jack and Mimi leaned in together to cut the cake, three snowy tiers decorated with fleurs-de-lis and gardenias and a ceramic couple under a bell. As the knife slid in, my father leaned toward my mother and asked through gritted teeth, "When will this goddamned bullshit be over?"

Mimi beamed for the photographer. Jack scowled, his contempt for convention recorded forever in their wedding album. When the party wound down, they took a taxi from Commonwealth Avenue to Back Bay Station and boarded the train to New York, the last stop before Bermuda. Boston-to-New York trains during the college season are endless rolling mobs of postadolescents. My parents were loaded with suitcases and high on champagne and possibility. They stood in the crowded vestibule between cars until somewhere in Connecticut, when two seats emptied. My mother was giddy with hope, my father made lighthearted by the reprieve from responsibility and tradition that had already begun to suffocate him.

After Bermuda, my parents settled in Philadelphia, where my father attended law school. While Dad studied, Mom learned to cook. They went out at night to see Nina Simone sing in a tiny jazz club. Mom went to work at the *Ladies' Home Journal*, where she sat in a bullpen with other young women, answering reader mail.

Jessica, Jack, Mimi, Harrisburg, Pennsylvania, 1960

Presented with questions like "How do I make *marrons glacés*?" "How do I set a formal table?" or "How can I learn about overpopulation?"—likely a secretive query about birth control—my mother chewed her pencil, visited the magazine's home economics department, and telephoned social service agencies. She typed her reply letters—every inquiry had to be answered—and sent them to the mailroom.

The Maxfield Parrish mural in the building's lobby showed blues and greens in dreamy light. On lunch breaks, my mother browsed bookstores or shopped for clothing at Wanamaker's with girlfriends from work. She punched a time clock, and collected her pay in cash.

In 1959, my father graduated from law school. He and my mother moved to his hometown of Harrisburg, where he joined his father's law firm. I was born in the fall, Susie less than two years later. In 1963, my father took a job as a field attorney for the National Labor Relations Board in its Detroit office. Having accepted the position, he sent my mother our new address via telegram: "CAN OCCUPY BY FEBRUARY FIVE. INVESTIGATE EARLIEST POSSIBLE MOVING DATES. LOVE JACK."

My mother packed up the house and left it for her in-laws to sell. With three-year-old me, baby Susie, and Willie the standard poodle, Mom flew to Detroit. The airline mistakenly shipped the dog to Chicago before discovering their error. The morning after our first night in our house, with furniture yet to arrive by moving van and a provisional breakfast from a nearby grocery on the counter, a yellow taxi pulled up to the snowy curb. The driver stepped out, walked a half circle around the nose of his cab, and opened the rear passenger door. Willie, his crate cast off somewhere in the Midwest, jumped down from the backseat into our flat front yard.

Our parents paid close attention to what delighted us. They avoided baby talk, addressing us in full sentences and expecting the same in return. My mother made our orange juice by pressing halved fruit in a metal juicer. I see now, in scrapbooks and boxes of letters and photos, that our pleasures were well-cataloged in letters to and from family and friends. Sometimes, we wrote to each other. "To the born one and her dear, dear mother, from their awed other half," my father wrote on a florist's card the day Susie was born. He signed it "Jessica and Jack." A lock of my hair is stored in an envelope marked "Jessica, 21 months." Drawings and cards scrawled in my beginner's print announce themselves in large letters, as if yelling. In Susie's, her hand was smaller and more determined to stay in the lines.

Susie and I were classical music buffs, even before I started kindergarten. Mom parked us in front of the TV with red boxes of animal crackers in our laps for an afternoon listening to Leonard Bernstein's Young People's Concerts. Afterward, while our recording of *Peter and the Wolf* wobbled on the turntable, Susie and I stalked around the house playing the bassoon grandfather and the clarinet cat.

When I was five, the snow in Detroit was often taller than my head. Dad dug out a canyon from our front door to his car at the curb. On a bright winter day, Susie and I wanted to go outside and play in the snow. I had been perched on my knees on a bench in front of the picture window in the dining room, watching two boys from up the street throw snowballs in their yard, hard. Their laughter floated toward me faster than the sight of their play—the sound was clear and sharp, and I heard it before one boy fell down in the snow, rose up, and pushed the other down. Like TV but more real, and in stinging, perfect color. Blue sky, white snow, yellow sun, red-plaid jacket on one of the boys, whom I knew by sight from the elementary school around the block, where I went to kindergarten, in Miss Laura's class.

The glass on the window was cold on my palms in front of me, and the house was warm behind me. Maybe I wanted to stay inside, but Susie insisted we go out. She was three.

"Let's get you girls wrapped up to go outside," Mom said, pulling scarves and hats from the closet by the front door. Susie ran toward her, a cannonball. I slid off my bench. I could taste the snow in my imagination, sweet and sharp, and I anticipated the frosty burn inside my nose when I got outside. I wanted even then to be big, able to just stroll outdoors without a coat heavy as a mattress on my back, without choking on too long scarves around my neck. I wanted to go outside and yell "Brrrr!" at the top of my lungs like Dad, walking fast to his car with his coat open, his bare hands jammed in his pockets.

Susie is already zipped into a snowsuit. Her arms and legs stick straight out, immobile. Mom wraps a scarf around her neck, once, twice, and tugs a fuzzy hat down over her ears before Susie waddles to the door. She reaches up, turns the handle, and looks back at Mom and me, calling, "Come on, Jessie, there's snow!"

Mom buttons me into a padded green-canvas jacket with red lining. She holds out snow pants with elastic straps under my feet for me to step into, one leg, then the other, and wraps a scarf around my neck, once, twice. Susie has the front door open, her nose against the glass storm panel on the screen door. Huff. She makes a circle of breath and draws a squiggle in it with her finger. Huff. I can't get my boots on; they're stuck on my bunched-up socks. I want to get outside and make a snow angel. The boys up the street are still shrieking and laughing. Their snowballs go "whump" when they hit.

Of the two of us, Susie is tenacious and I am ruminative. Susie could jump on the bed for longer stretches than I cared to. She created complex stories for her toys to act out. She sometimes fell asleep in a crouch, with her head down and hind end up, as if ready to spring into action at any moment. In photographs, I am often behind her, my hands on her shoulders. Wiry and energetic, Susie appears to be pulling away in pursuit of something more fun. Sometimes, her image is blurred.

When I am small, Dad smokes a pipe, like his father. He is tall and thin, and there is a sense of the daredevil around him. He listens to the hi-fi, loud, and we sing together to songs like "Abiyoyo," about a little boy who fells a giant. When his car breaks down, he pushes it home along Oak Park Boulevard, cursing and sweating in the summer heat.

When Willie the dog is sick, Dad stays in the basement with him all night, feeding him medicine and stroking his head. The dog has distemper, which I understand as a bad mood.

With my father, I learn to sound out the headlines in the newspaper. He takes me to the movies, and calls me "Jesserbaby." When he goes on business trips, he sends postcards to "the lovely ladies."

In the summers, Mom hangs clothes out on the line in the backyard, and I lie in the grass, listening to grasshoppers hit the dirt and feeling the sun on my face. On a hot afternoon when an airplane leaves a stripe in the sky that spreads after the plane moves out of sight, I cup my hands around my eyes to shield myself from the sun and to see only what's right in front of me, up in the faraway sky. I watch the stripe change into a benevolent curl before it widens and fades. It can't be there for no reason, a smile-shaped rip in the sky made by a plane.

"Mom, look," I say, pointing up. "It's God's teeth."

Susie and I play outside and act superior to the boys who live next door. They have light-colored hair cut short, like nailbrushes. Barclay and Jeremy come over to our yard every day in the summer—their mother drinks coffee in the kitchen with Mom, who by our second summer is pregnant. Susie and I dance around our backyard in Indian headdresses. We wear red-leather ankle bracelets with round bells.

"Hey yi yi yi!" I bellow, hopping on one foot and then switching to the other.

Susie follows me, chanting, "Hey yi yi yi."

She hops better than I do—she's not counting how many lefts and how many rights make a war dance. Both of us wear headdresses with white feathers that hang down our backs, gigantic things that our grandparents sent us from F. A. O. Schwarz in New York. We struggle for balance beneath their weight, certain that real Indians must dance looking down at grass and dirt.

Inside our peaked tepee, we eat sandwiches and Oreos and drink apple juice that looks like pee. The tented air is hot and makes us drowsy. Susie and I take a break from being Indians to watch ants crawl into the tent, deliberate and focused on their goal: a crumb of bread. Susie holds the tent flap open to make sure they can get home.

On summer nights indoors, I am Hercules. Over and over, with a blue-and-white dishtowel around my shoulders like the clothes the Mighty Hercules wears on television, I leap from the arm of the couch onto the floor and sing the chorus to the theme song "The Mighty Hercules!" The *e* at the end of *Hercules* gets drawn out, like a scream. I do this five or six times, getting farther out into space with every jump.

"For God's sake, stop that!" Mom calls from the bedroom, where she is getting Susie ready for bed. Mom doesn't know that when I jump off the cliff of the couch, just as Hercules leaps in every show, I am the hero of song and story, able to fight the evil Daedalus.

Sarah was born in January 1965, four days after the New Year. When Mom and Dad bring Sarah home from the hospital for the first time, Susie and I, in the care of our father's parents, have decorated our living room with a banner from Woolworth's. The banner is Grandma Rosalie's idea, and we are delighted with it, a strip of dangling shiny pink and purple and silver letters that spell out "Welcome Home."

When Dad's black Volkswagen grinds up to the curb, Susie and I watch him help Mom out of her door over mountains of snow. She cuddles a yellow blanket stuffed with a baby. We bounce up and down with joy and trip over each other racing for the kitchen door.

Inside, Grandma and Grandpa hug Mom and Dad and help them with their coats. Warm in the house, our parents look with wonder at the greeting taped to the doorjamb. We are a family of five.

Sarah is a blonde, solid baby with an elastic smile. Susie and I are both dark haired and leggy, but we three look alike when our faces are together. Mom calls us three peas in a pod. We cuddle Sarah like a toy, and she makes a growling sound, ramping up to eruptions of giggles. Dad calls her "Sarah Bearah" because of her rumbling noise. She is a sturdy baby, pleased with the world around her, and she rarely cries, despite the tubes of greasy antibiotics that litter her changing table.

4.

Susie . . . comes on like Barbra Streisand much of the time. She is capable of keeping a caterpillar as a pet for two months now, naming it Judy, [and] feeding it lettuce. . . . She is bony, good at cards, adept at the piano (if you want to hear variations on a theme of "I Wish I Were an Oscar Mayer Wiener").

—From a letter my mother
wrote to a friend, December 1968

Less than a year after voting rights activists Michael Schwerner, James Chaney, and Andrew Goodman—two white men and one black—were murdered in Mississippi, Mom found herself in the culturally uncharted South. Like adventurers of old, we had come to make our home, she said in amazement, "deeper south than South Carolina."

My mother was not worried for our safety. She was just thirty, and eager to experience a new way of life. We experienced no racial tension ourselves; our neighborhood and those surrounding it were almost entirely populated by white families, a product of custom and laws yet to come. I knew a few Cuban children, a few more from South America, and several from Greek families. The struggles in the larger world seemed to me separate from the evenly paced and smiling daily life in our neighborhood.

We moved to Atlanta in 1965 because my father believed he had a chance to change the world. He was the son of a lawyer who had become known among champions of social justice, a man who had argued and won a case before the U.S. Supreme Court in 1953. In the case, *Garner vs. Teamsters Union,* the Court upheld the rights of union members to picket for fair wages. A framed photograph of my victorious, smiling grandfather posing with his legal team on the mammoth steps of Chief Justice Earl Warren's Court was displayed in my grandparents' house in Harrisburg. A reverent hush signaled my grandfather's arrival into almost any room. His presence alone seemed to indicate that it was possible to fight injustice and win.

After two years in Detroit, my father took a job with the International Ladies' Garment Workers Union, the labor union that had become widely recognized in the aftermath of the Triangle Shirtwaist Fire in Manhattan in 1911. The union was a client of my grandfather's. My great-aunt Mary worked as a secretary in the union's New York office. Even before I started first grade, I knew to follow the instructions in the union's song, and *"look for the union label, in every coat, dress, or blouse."*

In the early 1960s, cotton grew outside towns in Georgia, the Carolinas, Alabama, and Mississippi. The mills and factories where workers wove, cut, and sewed the towels and sheets and shirts and pants made from that cotton drove much of the economy of the rural South. The union was eager to organize textile workers, many of whom were blacks and women getting their first opportunity for real employment the year the Civil Rights Act became law. The union came to fight inequity in the workplaces of the Jim Crow South. My father saw the southern labor movement as his opportunity to do what his father had done, and fight injustice in the world.

The year we arrived, Atlanta's Jewish population was fifteen thousand people, an increase of about one thousand from the prior year. The city's total population had just passed one million. That exuberant number sparkled from a sign made of lightbulbs at the entrance to a high-rise apartment building on Peachtree Road.

My mother wanted to see for herself the kinds of names the real estate agent promised her were on curbside mailboxes: Golden, Segal, Bergman. The Israeli consulate was in a house a few blocks away. The presence of other Jews promised that the intellectual tradition my parents knew existed in the foreign land below the Mason-Dixon line. My parents had not grown up attending synagogue beyond weddings, bar mitzvahs, and funerals, and they had no intention of starting now. Being Jewish was simply who we were, like being a family or being Americans or having ten fingers and ten toes. I had never heard any prayers, and had no formal Jewish education. My father simply trusted us to comprehend tyranny. Jews had experienced exile and contempt for thousands of years, he told me, although he gave no details. Jews knew slavery and Jews knew freedom, which made right-thinking Jews sympathetic to blacks.

My parents knew little Hebrew, and only casual Yiddish, which my father used primarily for cursing. *Schmatte*, a rag, as in a piece of clothing: what southern cotton was made into. *Dreck* was junk, as in my singing along with "Sugar, Sugar" by the Archies. Sometimes, for him, Yiddish described food, as in *schmaltz*, cooked chicken fat spread like jam across a slice of rye bread. Mom's sporadic Yiddish, in her Massachusetts-broad speech, was endearment. Watch your *keppi*—your head—when you ducked into the low doorway leading to the basement stairs. If I worried too much, I gave myself *tsuris*—troubles.

Dad loved life at the edge of the uncharted map. He looked like a young Gregory Peck, a loosely knotted tie around his neck, an unfiltered cigarette stuck to the right corner of his lower lip. In Atlanta, he and Mom went out at night with his friends, every one clever, every one agitated, dressed in Marimekko prints or floppy dashikis, and smelling of pot and patchouli. His friends included future mayors and ambassadors and other trim-Afroed, serious men, orbited by professors of social sciences, history, and literature. The sense of change in the air drew more friends; reporters decamped to the South to cover freedom marches and the effects of the new Voting Rights Act.

One morning when I was about seven years old, Mom clipped a short news item about a Ku Klux Klan rally from the *Atlanta Constitution* and taped it to a cabinet door. Stories like this one appeared periodically in the paper, and my mother viewed them as proof that we had moved to a foreign country. I no longer have the article, but newspaper archives yield others from the same period. One is datelined Stone Mountain, then a country town east of Atlanta where a three-acre relief carving was under way depicting Confederate generals riding the side of a mammoth granite hill. The morning paper reported that the meeting's speakers vilified Negroes, Jews, and President Johnson. Beside the article is a photograph of three Klansmen in hoods, saluting three crosses burning in the night. The item ran above an ad for Labor Day sales at Davison's department store.

For our part, Susie and Sarah and I absorbed southern accents easily. Mom, miffed by a bank teller's inquiring after her "chicken account," was unaccustomed to the foreign tongue. Dad took to the dialect easily after a hard start; for years he recounted the day he paled and backed away when a hostess at a reception waved ice tongs at him and sweetly asked if he cared for "a piece of ass."

My mother, who had not gone back to work after she had children, kept strong ties to her family outside the South, writing letters to her parents, her friends, and her brother. She smoked Parliaments while she wrote, winding paper into the typewriter's carriage before setting off tapping the keys as if she were racing.

"Sarah," she wrote, "is very sturdy, very brave, and very sick. I am capable of dealing with a temperature of 107 (I told her Goldilocks and helped the nurse sponge her down). Nothing upsets me anymore except the simple absence of a normal upset."

In the same letter, she exhorted her reader—the first page of the letter is lost, so I do not know to whom it was written or why a copy remains—to vote for Julian Bond, "for any office he chooses." In this way, Mom spread the news about life in the modern South, commenting on a young black member of the state legislature who had been a delegate to the 1968 Democratic Convention.

To me and Susie and Sarah, Atlanta was our home. When snow fell our first winter in Atlanta, the first graders in my class popped from their seats like wound springs and aimed for the window. I had seen snow before, heaps of it, but the silver sky and floating white flakes were a phenomenon for most of my classmates.

Whap! The teacher smacked a ruler against the top of her wooden desk. "Y'all git away from there!" she howled, truly fearful. "That stuff is radioactive, and it'll kill you."

Even though I knew better—in Michigan I had played in snow as tall as my mother's waist and hadn't yet gone radioactive—I skulked back to my seat along with everyone else. Maybe the snow in Georgia, the inch or so we would get every January that stuck to the grass for no more than a day, was tainted.

We had warm weather and long days most of the year— more time to play outdoors. Kids poured out of our brick-

and-tile school at recess: boys played kickball on the red-dirt playground, and girls clustered under the shade of pines to barter candy for Barbie outfits. A teacher balancing in a low-slung camp chair in the shade scattered us with a whistle blast, forcing the girls to get out onto the field and the boys to play nice. Morningside School's teachers tended to be lumpy ladies with cat-eye glasses who looked like LBJ in drag. We called our teachers "Ma'am," a reflexive, subservient gesture that drove my parents nuts.

Civil rights and the war drifted just over our heads. The only black people we encountered in school were Jim, the janitor who changed our lightbulbs and waxed the auditorium floor, and Lucy, who mopped up cafeteria vomit and puddles produced by kids not quite housebroken, quietly reassuring them that "it's all right, everything's all right."

There were no black students or teachers in my school until 1970, when two black boys, one tall, one short, appeared in my grade, and several black teachers were hired. As far as I could tell, the transition came easily.

In the late 1960s and the beginning of the seventies, the Vietnam War was as much a topic in our household as civil rights. Our portable black-and-white television sat on the edge of the kitchen table, and the images of helicopters in the jungle on the nightly news were often the backdrop to our dinner-table conversation. I was against the war because my parents were. Posters with peace signs decorated the wall over my bed. At school, the war was abstract, pushed out of my mind by the aggravation of the multiplication tables. When a third grader was hustled down the hall by the principal, rumor passed that her father had been killed in action. My classmates and I gaped, and were quiet and solicitous when she returned to school, afraid to bump into her in the cafeteria line or say the wrong thing, whatever that might be.

Mom didn't discuss the reasons that racism and violence were wrong. She left that to Dad, and to my scanning the newspaper headlines and absorbing the television news. At home, she created a world where she and her family would be happy, surrounded by beauty and growing things. In the spring, she knelt half-hidden behind sacks of mulch and a forsythia bush at the foot of the concrete birdbath in our yard.

Like the aphid spray for the white roses that climbed the wire fence in the backyard, the flower bulbs came from a store with a mascot: a live mynah bird. While Mom bought garden supplies, Susie and Sarah and I stood as close to the bird's tall cage as we could, eager to hear it speak.

"Pretty bird," we cooed. "Polly want a cracker?"

The bird eyed us suspiciously before answering in a matter-of-fact, and surprisingly deep woman's voice. The effect was fundamentally and wonderfully wrong, like that of a voice prompted by pulling the string on a talking doll.

"Birds can't talk!" the mynah scolded. The mynah cocked its stony black head. The bird had been taught to speak by a woman with a thick southern accent: *"cain't* talk," the bird said. We waited for this stock phrase every time, a bird punch line to a bird joke.

We laughed and tried again. Surely the bird would engage us in dialogue—ask what we liked for dinner, admire our haircuts.

Mom came up beside us, her packages paid for and bagged. "You can talk," she admonished the bird, conspiratorially. "You can't put one over on me."

The bird blinked at her and said nothing. We waited for this, too: Mom communing with a bird, elevating an animal to the status of peer.

. . .

Before she was two, Sarah was tormented by diaper rash and skin eruptions. Susie and I gagged at the sight of a scab on the pink curve of her belly, black and fissured like an olive pit. The crust capped the spot of a wick placed to draw fluid from an incision, relieving a new infection or an old one stirring deep under her skin. Sarah was clever and active, but sitting upright on her raw bottom made her cry.

Mom sensed that Sarah's doctor in Detroit had detected something. When he saw all of us in an office visit before we moved, he suggested to Mom that Sarah get a blood test as soon as we settled in Atlanta. There, Sarah was diagnosed with neutropenia, a general term for an abnormally low number of white blood cells. No cause was known, and Sarah was not expected to survive her childhood. Willing themselves into a normal life, Mom and Dad did not tell Susie and me; we were, after all, four and six.

Looking back today over my mother's archive of medical bills and correspondence is like fanning out decks of oversized, faded cards. No bills begin and end on the same page. Few correspondences are between only two doctors—most letters are copied to specialists in other practices. The first nine months of my parents' 1967 are recorded in a single thirty-page billing statement.

Medical-speak, like a third language, evolved in our house from the constancy of doctor visits and hospital trips. Sarah didn't just take medicine; she took Kantrex, Teramycin, Polymixin. On weekends, when I accompanied Dad to the dry cleaner, the bank, the delicatessen, and always the drugstore, he instructed me to remind him to "pick up the Chloro refill." (Chloramphenicol, a strong antibiotic for extreme infections, was to us as routine as sugar and common as milk, so customary that we referred to it in shorthand.)

When Susie and I had comparative blood work done, a measure of sisters that would be performed like clockwork for years, I knew our blood was being stripped and examined, spun down in a centrifuge or examined under glass. Dad got a copy of the *Physicians Desk Reference*, a hefty annual that weighed as much as the worn dictionary in the study. The slick pages showed color photographs wedged between column after column of tiny type. There were dizzying lists of benefits and side effects, dosages and manufacturers. The *PDR* was a kind of pornography, a siren song of delirium-inducing words and washed-out pictures of what could happen inside a body if provoked. Afraid of what I might read and unable to resist, I held my breath every time I stole a look at it.

Sarah learned to swallow her pills by practicing with hard candies. Mom tried sugar dots stuck to paper ribbons and individually wrapped tiny mints before she settled on gravel-hard Italian candy. Sarah washed her candy down with juice from a plastic cup. Susie and I lightened her load by swiping the candy from the tray of her high chair. We crunched down on what we grabbed, lemon and cherry flavors, rubbing our tongues against the sour fruit taste. Sarah ingested them whole and giggled in triumph.

• • •

On Saturday mornings, my father and I traveled the neighborhood together, doing errands that emphasized most of the ordinary things in our family's life. First, we shoved his suits through the drive-through window at the dry cleaner. Then, we went to the delicatessen and bought the food he liked: tinned sardines, glass jars of herring, and loaves of black bread. As an afterthought at the cash register, he often bought two dry white Halvah candy bars that tasted to me like chunks of sesame sawdust. Before we went home, we drove to the drugstore to collect the prescriptions Mom had called in.

If he was in a good mood, my father almost always made me drive when we were about two blocks from home.

"Here, hold the wheel." Dad lifted his hands away from the steering wheel. The car slowed but kept moving; his foot hovered over the accelerator. "Come on, I won't let us crash. You steer."

I told myself I wasn't afraid, and tried not to think about the cars that might be coming uphill as we went down, and the fact that I didn't know how to drive.

I balanced on my knees in the Volvo's passenger seat and leaned in for the wheel, while my father stretched his hands out toward the windshield. Until we were within a few feet of the two-lane traffic on Lenox Road and I begged my father to take control again, I was an adult. I held the car straight while my father rocked his foot heel to toe on the gas. I was terrified and thrilled. For a minute, I held our lives in my hands.

Dad took me with him on day trips in the summer and occasionally during the school year, short trips that I knew without being told were honorary. We drove to country towns around Atlanta—Newnan and Covington and Cartersville. Outside of Atlanta, the roads devolved from possum-gray asphalt to bloodred clay. We talked about school, about the relative merits of the Beatles versus the Monkees, about not being frightened about Sarah's being sick. I was almost eight. Outside the car's open window, green kudzu vines splayed over lonely houses like witch claws.

This was one of the few times that my father attempted to broach the subject of our family, medicine, and doctors, but I didn't want to talk about Sarah. I wanted the private time of being the only daughter with my father, traveling through the world outside our home.

When we got to our destination, we pulled off the road, bumped over ruts, and rolled to a stop, often in a field of beaten-down grass. Almost instantly, Dad was surrounded by ropy black men in overalls and serious women in print dresses. They talked with him under pecan trees or on the front steps of their homes, cooling their faces with the paper fans that came as giveaways from funeral parlors and appliance stores.

Dad wore a suit and tie to meet the people he called "the rank and file," a phrase he uttered with the solemnity other men used when they said "amen" at the end of a prayer. He bent his head and conversed with them in a deferential way.

Between sips of sweet tea from metal cups or scrubbed-out jars, I said, "Thank you, ma'am" and "Pleased to meet you, sir" to elbows and knees that rushed off to get their time with my father. Sometimes they dragged their own staring children away from me, the only white child for miles, the only child in a mod culottes outfit patterned with sunflowers. My clothing looked perfect when I left Atlanta, but was awkward here, where groovy was meaningless.

On our way home I sang the song about the Union Maid, who never was afraid, *"of the goons and the ginks and the company finks, and the deputy sheriffs who made the raid."* In my imagination, I was the valiant Union Maid, and nothing could keep me down. My father, steering a company car with his nicotine-stained index finger, loosened his tie and imagined himself Atticus Finch.

I no longer know the names of the mills and factories where these men and women worked or wanted to work; most no longer exist. My father may have been taking depositions or explaining union benefits to potential members.

He surely told me on those trips why we were visiting, or what he thought was unjust about the rules a company was attempting to enforce, but these dry facts burned away on my hot afternoons in the country. What mattered most about these adventures with my father was my inclusion in an adult world my sisters were too young for.

In the few years before the fight to save my sisters' lives overwhelmed him, my father glittered with energy. In the mid-1960s, a photographer took a picture of him sitting inside a courtroom in Wake County, North Carolina. In it, he is no more than thirty-five years old. With his arm slung over the back of the bench where he waits during a break, he looks expansive, confident, watchful—a man in charge. My father took pride in representing the underdog in an unfair world.

One afternoon in a small-town courtroom, a man in overalls approached my father curiously.

"Mr. Handler, I hear you're a Jew," the man said.

"That's right," Dad answered.

(I can imagine his voice, measured and low.)

A shade belligerent, the man asked, "Can I feel your head?" He pronounced it *"hayid."*

When Dad told me this story later, he explained that he leaned forward and let the man's fingers probe carefully through his dark hair. He was, Dad explained, feeling for horns.

Even though I was a child, my parents believed that I could absorb knowledge about the world beyond our home. I had already read newspaper headlines and eaten my dinner to the backdrop of the evening news. I had heard conversations about racism and rights in the workplace. I am sure that because of this, I was allowed to watch the world change that spring.

I saw my first dead body when I was eight years old. In the early evening of April 4, 1968, I was sitting on the floor watching a Woody Woodpecker cartoon. When the newsbreak interrupted my show, I knew that if I didn't tell what I had heard right away, I would be in big trouble. In stocking feet, I hopped up and slid into the kitchen in a run. Mom was sweeping the floor.

"Hey, Mom, does Dad know somebody named Dr. Martin Luther King?" I spoke all seven syllables of his name jammed together as if they were one word.

She put the broom aside, and gave me a quizzical look. Yes, she answered. I knew that some of Dad's friends had gone to Memphis earlier that week, intending to put their support or their good intentions behind the months-long sanitation workers' strike there.

"I think Dr. King got shot," I said. I felt as if I were waving my arms to capture my balance on the edge of the adult world. Mom reached for the phone.

Dad took me to King's funeral the following Tuesday. Mom agreed with him that my going was part of my social legacy. Susie and Sarah were too young to attend.

Reading news clippings today gives me perspective on the event my father allowed me to see. That day, he was quiet and spoke almost in a whisper, even before we entered the church. His step wasn't heavy for a tall man, but he usually moved hard, sitting with enough force that couch cushions tumbled to the floor, or grinding his car's gears when he drove. That day, my father moved gently. We were two people of more than one hundred thousand to fill Auburn Avenue, a busy street that extended from the historically black business district west into downtown. All were on foot, and some held black umbrellas open to shade themselves from the sun. Mourners crossed the threshold of Ebenezer Baptist Church alone, or in twos and threes. Inside, the sunlight and the electric light mixed together, making a yellow glow. News cameras whirred in the springtime heat. When we reached the casket after what seemed like an hour or more, my father lifted me high above the lip of the casket so that I could pay my respects to Dr. King.

For a moment, I was mesmerized. I could see now that he had not been tall. I had watched him on television, speaking to crowds, shining with sweat. His face was round, and here, close enough to touch, his skin was oddly dusted and dry. After just a minute suspended over the coffin, I wanted urgently to be set down. The elastic waistband of my dress pinched my skin, and my father's thumbs dug into my armpits, pushed there by his awkward support of my weight. My father put me down, and we walked forward with the slow crowd, moving out of the church door, past the green wooden farm wagon and the harnessed mules waiting to take Dr. King's body away.

5.

"Now then!" the Badger said heartily. "Tell me the news from your part of the world."

—*The Wind in the Willows*

As children, Susie and Sarah and I were entranced by animal stories like *The Wind in the Willows* and *The Tale of Peter Rabbit*. We wanted to be Peter Rabbit's friend and ride in a boat with Mole. Sarah got Richard Scarry's picture books when they were new, and traced her fingers on the oversized pages where anthropomorphic mice flew planes and dogs directed traffic. Animals in our household were almost equal to people, an entertainment and a delight. We participated in the world more fully by dancing with the dog, or staring into a knocked-over metal trash can in the driveway to see the mother possum that had crawled inside with her brood.

When Susie and I were six and eight, we got an ant farm, but the first ants were dead. Susie dumped them from their container onto the narrow shelf of sand, where they lay, reddish brown, shiny, and motionless. Some ants lay on their backs, legs up. Those were certainly goners. We could have drawn Xs over their eyes, they were so dead. The ones who landed facedown, in a position approximating life, seemed more likely to reincarnate or otherwise come to their senses and begin carving the tunnels they were born to dig. We hung our hopes on the ones we presumed would be survivors.

Cooing and murmuring encouragement, Susie and I tapped on the green plastic barnyard shapes crowning the ant farm. Ant farms were a trendy toy that season, slices of life about half the size of a record album jacket and the width of a slice of toast. A captive insect colony was one more way to have pets. As a family, we delighted in surrounding ourselves with living things we could adore and imbue with semihuman characteristics. Willie, our dog, had become an honorary person (Mom taught him to smile on command and to dance on his hind legs), and Dad brought a kitten home, an orange male tabby with a sour demeanor whom Susie insisted on naming Alice. I had named my hamster Paul, in honor of the cute Beatle.

Susie and I shook the ant farm's frame side to side, like the yawing of a boat, shuffling the inert bugs deeper into the white sand. They remained wedged in position, like grains of rice inside a saltshaker.

A parent or grandparent must have ordered replacement ants, because a new package of insects arrived in the mail. They withstood Susie's swift upending of their traveling container into new sand, and set to work homesteading as soon as they planted their feet on their arid farm. They industriously tunneled nowhere, pushing sparkling flecks up tiny hills. Once they got working, I found I couldn't watch them. Peering at activity usually performed beneath the earth and transplanted to what amounted to a picture window, I felt I had become an ant Peeping Tom. While they worked, I buried my nose in a book, embarrassed. They farmed away on Susie's bureau while we slept. In the morning, she gently carried their miniature muleless forty acres into her second-grade classroom for show-and-tell.

While Susie tended her ant farm, I had become horse-crazy. On occasional Saturday afternoons, I persuaded my father to take me to a nearby stable. While I sat on a fat pony with a saddle as broad as our kitchen double sink, Dad held the reins and walked beside me. Traveling at the pony's numbingly sullen pace, I waved at drivers on Briarcliff Road, then waved at teenage stable hands, and then came back around to wave at a new burst of cars escaping the traffic light. Even though we were blocks from the medical complex at Emory University, a few minutes' drive from Atlanta's first upscale shopping mall, and I could glimpse our dog's veterinarian's office through the trees, in my mind, I was leading a parade through an Old West town. No hands but mine held the doddering pony in check.

The pony ring wasn't enough for me. My father's friend, a union organizer in South Carolina, owned a few horses. I fell hard for one of them the first time we went to visit. I called her "Tammy," liberating her from some unromantic name, and rhapsodized about her in my diary. Feeling sporty and reckless, I hung over the paddock gate to offer her apples and carrot sticks. In a full sideways split, I sat on her back while she walked beside her fence, led by an indulgent adult holding her bridle. From then on, I told my goggle-eyed friends in Atlanta that I had a horse. We kept her, I said airily, "up in South Carolina."

On one of our trips to the South Carolina farm, Susie sagged against the car door, submerged in sleep. Briefly awakened by bumps in the road or stops at service stations, she kicked the back of Mom's seat and complained. Sarah sat between us, belted in and waving my hand-me-down stuffed tiger in the air. Dad drove and smoked.

When we arrived, Mom guided sleepwalking Susie into the house, shuffling behind her with both hands on her shoulders. She put Susie to bed in the guest room, patting her hot forehead with a cold washcloth. She had undoubtedly picked up the flu somewhere, Mom told Dad's friends, what with summer camp and the germ warfare that kids' birthday parties can be. Leave her to sleep, and I'll check on her every few hours.

I rode Tammy, while Susie stayed in the house, sick.

The night we got back to Atlanta, I was depressed because the law had been laid down during the drive home: no, for the last Goddamned time, I could not have a real horse at home. Susie slumped at the dinner table. She was as white as the moon. Lavender streaks like mimeograph ink curved under her eyes. Normally, she tore around the house in one of Mom's discarded nightgowns and pumps from our dress-up box, screeching to a halt to slam shut an open cabinet drawer or smooth out a rippled rug. Susie liked action and she liked order.

"Stand up so I can get a good look at you," Mom said.

She spoke in the same deceptively offhand tone she used to remind us to place our napkins in our laps. The skin on Susie's arms and legs was flecked with inky pinpoints. More purple speckled her back and chest. Mom pulled Susie's T-shirt up over her ribby sides. Fork in hand, still chewing, Dad pushed away from the table and went to the kitchen phone. He dialed our pediatrician at home, a privilege he considered his right. Howard (the honorific "Doctor" had long since been discarded) told Dad to bring Susie to the hospital. He would meet them there and take a look.

Susie balked at seeing the doctor, even though she had barely been able to lift her head from beside her plate. *Bewitched* was going to be on in a few minutes, and we always watched it together. Leaving the house in a hurry to see the doctor wasn't new, but hustling anyone but Sarah off in the night felt wrong, and frightening. Mom laced up Susie's Keds, wiped her mouth, and packed her off with Dad. It wouldn't take long to go see Howard, she promised. I wanted to go, too. I was bucking for a chance to stay up late, unfamiliar with the new feeling of being cast aside.

"Help your mother," my father instructed. His voice was stern.

Doctors say that expecting the worst diagnosis before you have proof is hearing hoofbeats and expecting zebras, not horses, a reminder to look for the ordinary before you search for something strange. With Susie's illness, my father believed that zebras were thundering up to our door. Angered by his readiness to embrace disaster, my mother argued with him. That night, while I slept, my parents began the slow and terrible turning away from one another that erodes families facing the death of a child. My father became heart. My mother became mind.

This widening rift was almost impossible to detect by anyone outside the ring of our family. Because Mom insisted that life was beautiful and would always stay safe, we tried to believe it was true. This same year, my mother was the PTA chair for Morningside School, convincing neighborhood mothers to save piles of outdated newspapers for a fund-raising paper drive. I took piano lessons, clarinet lessons, and ballet lessons, and had to be driven a dozen different places for recitals and reeds and blue or pink leotards, colors signifying my membership in the Thursday or Saturday dance class. Sarah had learned to walk by pushing herself along behind a child-size chair, and she navigated the house at high speeds, using her red Mexican folk-art chair as a walker.

Even with my mother's focus on moving forward, Sarah knew everything wasn't fine. As a toddler, she named an unloved doll "Body," and for the most part ignored it. If an adult asked to see the doll, she usually refused. "Can't," Sarah would say. "Body is sick."

Even at two or three years old, Sarah must have known intuitively that she was not separate from her body or the ways in which it troubled her.

I understood Sarah's illness as an integral part of her selfness, part of the package that made her my sister. I did not know her prognosis—I did not know the word—and I did not ask.

Susie and Sarah and I had begun the habit of climbing on our mother after dinner and rocking from side to side in a slow rhythm, hugging one another tightly and smelling of shampoo and toothpaste. Together, we sang a four-note song we had made up to name our ritual.

"Loving party, loving party," skipping across the piano keys from F to C to A and back to F, one note for each syllable.

From deep inside this knot of females, Susie was inspired one night to sing out a Dadaist counterphrase in a mock baritone. "Swimming in the trees," she sang, rippling down the scale, GFEDC.

· ˙ ·

I don't remember my father coming home that night without Susie, or waking up the next morning and seeing my sister's bed untouched, but I know that for the first time in my life, I felt uneasy. My sister's chair at the kitchen table was empty, and I looked away. Her bed stayed made, and I meticulously kept myself from tossing my schoolbooks, socks, or hairbrush on it, because suddenly Susie's bed without Susie took on a huge importance. The empty bed was a threat. Treat this wrong, and Susie might not come back to it. Treat it right, and when you turn around, she might be here.

In the morning, Mom and Dad left for the children's hospital, leaving Sarah and me with a sitter. I imagine now that Susie must have slept poorly after being put to bed in a hospital room with striped curtains and a bedpan on the nightstand. Rubber-soled shoes squeaking down linoleum hallways during the night replaced the sound of a dog's sleeping sighs.

Mom and Dad took shifts over what must have been several days keeping Susie company and waiting for news. Mom took the cold vinyl chair by Susie's bed and surely worked hard to entertain her, telling stories and changing channels on the wall-mounted television. Dad paced from the elevator to the nurses' station, waiting and watching for Howard. Sick with fear, Mom and Dad changed places every few minutes.

My mother tells me that during one rotation she nearly collided with Howard at the elevator. He had been crying. He held a manila folder with lab reports in his hand. My mother's first reaction, in the cotton-wool silence of that moment, was to stare at his red-rimmed eyes. Insulated by denial, Mom wondered why she had never before noticed Howard's allergies. The zebras my father had imagined had arrived.

Howard was a family friend. Susie and Sarah and I played with his children. The three adults may have stepped into the hallway or gone to the nondenominational chapel near the lobby to talk. They did not discuss how long Susie would live; they each understood that everyone would do everything they could.

Susie had developed a cancer identified by overproduction of white blood cells. Paired with Sarah's illness, a diagnosis of leukemia was a coincidence that did not escape the notice of doctors or my parents. Susie's body had spontaneously begun producing too many white blood cells, while Sarah's consistently produced too few. In later years, Mom named this synchronicity a "reverse miracle," a phenomenon that for all its power to amaze the medical community generated no blessing for the family that bore it.

No one ever told Susie just how sick she was, or explained to her that she had cancer. No one told me for almost a year. She and I knew she was changing, doing something and going somewhere without me, but as second and third graders, we had no words for what would happen.

"I had a bad dream," Susie whispered across our dark bedroom, months after she was diagnosed.

Her bed was on one side of the window, mine on the other. We had matching Indian-print bedspreads that smelled vaguely of incense, the scent of the avant-garde shop where Mom had bought them. In the moonlight, the beige paisley looked like flesh.

"What was it?" I whispered back.

Susie dreamed of a wooden rocking chair that rocked back and forth on a porch, hard enough to make the floorboards creak. The chair was empty, but it moved furiously, with the energy of someone invisible sitting in the slatted seat. The chair rocked and rocked all by itself, scaring Susie so much that she woke herself up to escape the image.

"That's a creepy dream," I agreed.

We both lay awake on either side of the window. The dog whiffled and sighed in his sleep on the cotton rug between our beds. Our parents slept lightly in their room down the hall, and Sarah's room, linked to ours by a bathroom, hummed with the small motor of her humidifier.

Susie's hair fell out from chemotherapy. Without a word about the loss, Mom got Susie a brown wig. Wigs for adult cancer patients may have been easier to get. A wig for a seven-year-old was neither easy to find nor easy to bear. Wrapping her head in a scarf was worse. Susie looked sunken and eerily like a tiny immigrant ancestor turned back at Ellis Island for contagion.

Some days fragile and others burning with energy, Susie started third grade in remission from cancer. On the school yard was the only place I protected her, powered by my own anger and frustration. The force of my rage made my eyes tear and the skin on my arms crawl with fury. I was rabid with anger and passion, and shocked by the force of my emotion.

Our classes took recess at the same time, and even before she was sick, I always looked for Susie on the playground, trying to make up for what I considered arbitrary daytime separation by our teachers. One day an older boy, alert to her wig because it had gone cockeyed, ran past and knocked it into the red dust. The curly pile of hair lay like a woodland animal for barely a second before a group of sympathetic little girls snatched it up and formed a semicircle around Susie. They wiped the hair clean on their shirts, while a teacher knelt and placed the wig neatly back atop Susie's head. Susie didn't move, not quite believing she had actually been denuded in public.

"You *putz!*" I shrieked at the boy, a knobby-kneed stranger.

The word, a cuss that Dad used, had no meaning for me; it was simply the worst thing I could think of to call a boy. A girl could not be a *putz*. Under his breath, Dad called careless lab technicians and arrogant bosses *putzes*. To be a *putz* meant you were ignorant and selfish, devoid of

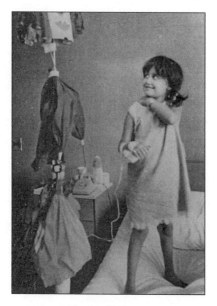

Susie, Atlanta

sophistication. I took off across the playground, running fast enough to make my sides ache. Before I could tackle the culprit, he was absorbed into a pack of preteen boys by the green wooden seesaws.

Pudgy and unathletic, I limped back to where Susie sat on a bench, making yarn cat's cradles with her friends.

"Are you okay?" I gasped, feeling mean, hating my slow body as much as I hated the galloping boy.

"Yeah, I'm okay," Susie said.

Her wig had a false shine, like doll hair. Susie turned back to weaving yarn with her fingers, making the Jacob's ladder that I could never get right.

. ˙ .

When Susie wasn't in the hospital, she had weekly blood tests, quick visits to the doctor's office in hours wedged between school and playdates with friends. The rise and fall of her blood count reported over the phone by a lab tech to Mom on Monday mornings would dictate the remainder of our family's week. Dad contacted various medical colleges that might be researching genetic illnesses. Maybe they could offer more information. My father wrote to the University of Wisconsin, and sent abstracts of Sarah's medical chart and the results of Susie's weekly blood work to Duke University.

In July 1969, the five of us flew to Durham for a series of blood tests that might reveal the origin of our reverse miracle. Sarah and Susie and I were accustomed to flying and the accompanying marvel of sitting down to breakfast in one city and to lunch in another. We flew to New York to visit great-aunts, doting women who took us to puppet shows, museums, and Central Park. We ate with chopsticks in Chinatown and spent nights in homes unlike our own: compact apartments with tiny kitchens and imposing brownstones with backyard gardens. In the summer, we went to Pennsylvania and sometimes to Massachusetts to see grandparents.

Traveling to Duke was just another visit to another hospital. We were prepared to fulfill our responsibility to more doctors—interchangeable with the ones at home—and to our parents before we got to play around the motel pool or dress up to go out for dinner. We were polite. We presented the insides of our arms, sleeves rolled up, for the needle. We gently flicked our fingers against the insides of our elbows to raise the big vein there, showing off just a little bit for the lab tech. Our frankness made her stare. We answered questions: how old we were, how we were feeling, what Sarah's stuffed bear was named.

Thinking I was being helpful, I confided in the doctor, a blonde woman who appeared no older than the nursing student who babysat us at home. "I'm the well sibling," I announced to her as I shook her hand, attempting to clarify who was who.

After each of us relinquished vial after vial of blood and my parents completed pages of paperwork, we left the lab. Susie fainted while we waited for the elevator. When she crumpled to the floor, my parents' calm shattered: Mom screamed, Dad swore, and a male lab tech in white came running. I was afraid. As sick as I knew Susie and Sarah were, any real evidence of their weakness or fallibility had always been confined to the days when they were patients in a hospital. No one ever fainted, threw up, or bled in street clothes.

Susie spent her eighth birthday in the hospital. I recorded the day in my scrapbook, drawing a picture of the bar of perfumed soap I gave her as a gift. Above it I added, "Susie had some cake with me."

On the way into the hospital, after I had ritually stomped on the mat that triggered the automatic sliding doors, my parents and I walked through the gleaming lobby. We routinely defied the "no visitors under twelve" rule, and as we passed the reception desk the woman at the switchboard nodded and waved. I carried Susie's cake in a white bakery box. Egleston Children's Hospital had a courtyard garden with benches and paved paths, accessible through the glass doors across the lobby from the front door. There, white sculptures like mastodon ribs curved skyward in the sculpture garden. Wearing a summer dress, Susie curled into the slope of one of the mysterious bones after finishing her slice of cake.

6.

Clinical situation continued to deteriorate. . . .
At 24 hrs. prior to demise, she developed congestive
failure.

—Henrietta Egleston Hospital for Children, Inc.
[Final] Discharge Summary, Susannah Jenny Handler,
November 13, 1969

Early in the fall that I turned ten, Dad asked me to come into the kitchen after Susie and Sarah had gone to bed. Over the past months, he had become a banger and a slammer, angry at the world. Tonight, though, he gently closed the doors that led to the hallway, the dining room, and the family room, walking a semicircle and trapping me in the kitchen with him and Mom. I knew that Susie was sick, that both my sisters took pills, and that they were in and out of the hospital and doctors' offices. We had been to Duke and had our blood drawn. I attributed sickness to who we were as a family, but no one had yet talked to me about death.

In the kitchen, Mom remained standing, her hands pressed flat against the countertop, her head hanging. Dad sat in a chair at the table, and motioned for me to sit beside him. The window over the sink exposed the completely black night.

"I have something very hard to tell you, and I want you to know that you are old enough to hear this," he said, looking closely at me.

Frightened, I chewed my lower lip and longed, for the first but not the last time in my life, to have the power to make time run backward.

I looked at Mom. Her eyes were wet, but her lips were set in a firm line. Her chin dimpled like a peach pit, her jaws working against crying. Dad waited for me to look back at him.

"Susie has a disease called acute lymphocytic leukemia. She's going to die, Jessica. We don't know when, but it will happen soon, maybe in a few months."

Dad was crying, but he did not wipe his tears. I heard him tell me that they were doing everything they could for Susie, and that her doctors were working very hard. He told me to treat her normally and to love her. Indignant, I thought, I do that anyway.

The rhyming vowel sounds of *leuk* in *leukemia* and *cute* in *acute* pounded in my head. Craving the shelter of a small space, I moved off my chair and crouched on the floor, my head under the table and my back against the door. My fa-

ther told me later that I screamed, but I remember only silence and then the sound of the pill bottles rattling in his
pockets as he knelt in front of me. My mother stayed by the
sink, frozen with grief. Dad opened my mouth with his fingers and placed a pill on my tongue, probably a barbiturate.
He told me to swallow hard. He knew I did not need water.
(All of us girls were pros at taking pills by now, Susie and
Sarah by necessity and me because I couldn't stand that
they could do something I couldn't. In the mornings, I swal-
lowed my vitamins without juice, wishing that they meant
more.)

Try to sleep, Dad said, and know that this is not your
fault. I knew it wasn't: how could a disease be anyone's
fault?

The last time I saw Susie was after midnight two months
later, in our bedroom. She woke up crying, and Mom tiptoed into our room to check on her. Half-asleep and trying
to stay that way, I jammed a pillow around my head. I
squinted my eyes shut against the light snapped on in the
room. Susie and Dad were on their way to the hospital,
again. I said good-bye, feel better. Susie was crying, and I
don't know if she heard me. Dad whispered for me to go
back to sleep, and he shut off the light.

I spent the next week and a half in my own routine. I
went to bed and woke up in a bedroom that was only half-
occupied. I imagined a painted line on the floor dividing
our room in two, and offered a silent and general apology if
I had to cross it to get to my closet or out the door. I began

to be late for school around this time, dawdling until I heard the television news announcer tell me that it was "8:25 and time for Georgia news and weather." With five minutes to go, I would never make it in time, but the world kept going.

Walking to and from school, I kept my sights on the sidewalk, watching out for cracks. To avoid them, I took overlong steps, or short ones, or walked along the grass at the edge of the concrete. If I lost my balance or otherwise landed my weight on a crack, I started over on a smooth space. I couldn't give this up, no matter how late it made me.

In the afternoons, I did homework and watched television. I am sure I asked about Susie. I am sure my parents said that she asked about me. I am sure we talked on the phone, but not about much. Retelling who had a birthday party or how much homework I had felt uncomfortable and mean. I could not have explained it then, but recounting the normal events of my daily life to Susie, suspended from hers, felt as if I were showing off. Merely by having a school day, I experienced moments missing from her life.

Susie's absence had become nearly normal, as had my parents' coming and going at odd hours. This was the way we lived, and for my part, I did my best to be unobtrusive. It was the least I could do.

Ten days after Dad made his late-night run to the hospital with Susie, I heard Mom early one morning coaching Sarah through getting dressed.

"Stick your leg out straight," she told Sarah, who made herself laugh by putting her pants on her head.

My parents had appeared only in brief shifts during the preceding week, coming home to leaf through piles of mail or give grocery money to the cheerful nursing student who had been our babysitter and cheerleader for several years. For a fraction of a second I couldn't place my mother's voice: the flat New England vowels and gentle rhythm were familiar, and a feeling of love overwhelmed me when I heard them. If Mom was home, Susie must be better.

"Mom, how's Susie?" I yelled, sitting up in bed.

"I'll be right there," Mom called, muffled by the wall.

When she came in, my mother sat gingerly on the edge of my bed. She looked at the closet door, the row of plastic horses on the bookshelf, the "War Is Not Healthy for Children and Other Living Things" poster.

"Susie died last night," Mom said. "Peacefully."

She sounded rehearsed, as if she were mouthing the words to a language she did not know. She smelled of her trademark patchouli, and when she reached out to hug me, she felt fragile and distant, as if she were leaning into me and pulling away at the same time.

Dad was "taking care of things" at the cemetery. As Mom stood to leave my room, the one rabbi we knew appeared. We had attended his new synagogue in Atlanta a few times, but going to religious services was a spiritual experiment for my parents quickly derailed by the extreme demands on their time and their faith.

The rabbi talked to me softly about loss and how my mother and father still loved Sarah and me, and how they would always love Susie, too. Through my hands, I stared down at his shoes, black wing tips scuffed near the heels. Focusing on them kept me from diving under the bed. I knew that I was supposed to cry, but I couldn't. Instead, I felt panic.

For the first time, I felt abandoned. I knew Susie had been sick for more than a year. I had been told that she was going to die. I was ten years old, and death was not a clear concept in my mind.

Not crying, knees up under my chin and arms around my ankles, I made my mind wander as the rabbi spoke. I searched for some tragic idea that would force me to cry. Ships lost at sea. Dogs at the pound. Hungry children in Biafra. Suddenly, I imagined a plate of doughnuts. Picturing the poor doughnuts with holes in their middles finally brought tears.

The first snow fell during Susie's funeral, early in the year for Georgia. My parents, my four grandparents, and I were driven to the cemetery in a funeral-home limousine. A babysitter stayed home with Sarah, who was four. We took our seats in the first row of metal folding chairs arranged on the grassy hill in front of Susie's open grave. When the rabbi from the day before began his service, I stared hard at a monument on the hillside opposite us, determined to fight the ache rising in my throat. I shoved my hands in my coat pockets and curled my toes inside my shoes, trying to lift them away from the cold ground. The rabbi spoke in English and then in Hebrew, but I could hear only my heartbeat and my own breathing. Dad had told me that the dead live on forever in our thoughts. I tried not to think of what Susie might look like inside her coffin. Mom had dressed her in a long sky-blue cotton nightgown. Were Susie's hands folded or by her sides? I wondered. Was she wearing her wig?

From my left came a sharp jab in my side.

"Hold your mother's hand," my father hissed. He gestured almost imperceptibly toward my mother beside me. The elbow poke came again, hard enough to make me gasp. Through his teeth, he made a demand. "Cry, damnit."

For the past day, I had shadowed my mother around the house, chewed the ends of my hair, and was afraid to let Sarah out of my sight, but I had not cried. My parents were too busy with their tasks to talk; they made phone calls, they came and went from the house, grandparents arrived.

My father's poke in my side transformed my grief into anxiety. I know now that his expectation was for me to step up to the miniadult role I had taken during our country drives, and to help him shoulder his burden by demonstrating my own sorrow.

We came home to find that our neighbors had organized a meal with enough leftovers to last into the week. Mom was flustered by the attention. She insisted through hug after hug that she could prepare our dinner and that everything would go on just fine, thank you for coming, and please don't trouble yourselves. She looked dazed and small. Howard ran a tall glass of water for her from the kitchen tap and handed her a sedative before he sent her to bed.

Dad said little. He sat in the family room and looked out the window, at the grass turned yellow and dusted with snow, at the cap of ice on the concrete birdbath.

In our dining room, the table leaves had been pulled out and linen runners laid down by friends and neighbors performing what Emily Dickinson called the "bustle in a house," an attempt to fend off the collapse of small things that so often attends grief. Casseroles, brisket, cookies, and ambrosia salad crowded the table, and one woman—someone's mom from PTA—poured coffee from the percolator into mugs and Mom's little-used antique cup-and-saucer sets.

Sarah, small even for four, was passed from lap to lap, hugged and kissed, and encouraged to play with the scarves and necklaces she reached for. My littlest sister was a welcome distraction for sorrowful guests, too young to understand the reason for the assembly. She welcomed their attention.

I sat for a while with one grandmother and then the other, moving absently between two perfumes. The air around me felt brittle. I had nothing to do with my hands, and nothing to say to the people who hugged and petted me. My mother was in bed in the middle of the afternoon. I slipped out to the front yard and paced in the oval track I had begun to wear into the grass.

Inside, my family began slowly to float away.

7.

I saw you in the ocean / I saw you in the sea / I saw
you in the bathtub / whoops! Pardon Me!

—Jessica's end-of-year autograph book, 1970

The first step in not talking about what had happened to us
after Susie died was to take a family vacation. Too many
hospital trips had come to mean less time and money and
inclination to act with abandon. The last time we piled as a
group into the car, with sunglasses and silly songs and sandwiches in a cooler, was before we left Detroit for Atlanta,
when all five of us went in Mom's red Rambler station
wagon on a big loop east, visiting cousins and grandparents.
Since then, we had made short visits to family up North,
and I had gone with Dad to Florida several times, playing at
the hotel pool with the kids of his work friends while he
went to labor union meetings. The summer after Susie

died, my father and Howard rented a sprawling, run-down house in Jamaica.

After Susie's death, Mom and Dad moved through their days slowly, as though the act of motion caused them physical pain. Dad smoked more, unfiltered Pall Malls that seemed stuck to his lower lip or between his fingers. Mom's gestures were abrupt and her shoulders hunched. Sarah and I went back to school.

Less than a month after Susie died, I heard her voice coming from the kitchen. She was laughing, just a blip of sound, but completely alive. I flung the bedroom door open and tore down the hall.

"Stop it!" I yelled, unsure if I was shushing my sister's ghost or if someone was playing a terrible joke.

Mom sat at the kitchen table, a small pile of Susie's books and clothing folded in front of her, a tape player in her lap.

"Turn it off! Turn it off!" I stood weeping in the kitchen, frantic from the sound of my sister's disembodied voice.

Mom stopped the tape. She was red-faced, as if she had been caught in an illicit act. Even as she apologized to me, I felt ashamed of my reaction. She should have been able to listen to her child's voice again.

. . .

Time in Jamaica must have seemed like a solution to Dad: all water and sun to wash away our troubles. He envisioned making sand castles on the shore, buying crafts in open-air markets, and eating fresh fruit on a shady veranda. His urge to escape our surroundings overshadowed our collective need. Mom, Sarah, and I needed to stay in a place we knew, redefining together what our family would be like without Susie. Instead, we bought swimsuits.

Vacations are about togetherness, but even then, our family's trip to Jamaica felt forced, and I felt guilty. Traveling without Susie was traitorous. I couldn't point out the deception to Mom and Dad; we were engaged in a troop movement well beyond my friends' trips to Miami Beach or Disneyland. This was privilege, something I knew Dad would remind me that I should be grateful for.

Howard had been our family pediatrician since we arrived in Atlanta. He had treated Susie and Sarah before they were handed over, one by one, to specialists. He had wept openly at our kitchen table about my sisters. He stayed up nights with Dad in our den, drinking, smoking, and fuming. In his examining room, he convinced me to close my eyes and think of Hershey bars as a distraction while he administered my school vaccinations.

Howard and his wife had two sons, almost the exact ages as Sarah and me. At ten years old, I snubbed the boys, sure that I was being forced to befriend them because Howard and Dad were so close.

Some weekend afternoons we drove to the prim, landscaped neighborhood where Howard and his family lived. I sat on their gleaming living room floor and read the older son's *Mad* magazines to pass the time. Being friendly made me tired. It was easier for me to puzzle over the oblique, wordless *Spy versus Spy* comic strip. I wanted to spend my waking hours reading about lives other than my own. Sarah sharpened her nascent skill for palling around primarily with boys, bossing the younger son over hands of Old Maid or exploring their backyard.

In Jamaica, the house's pool was a concrete trough filled hip-deep with stagnant brown water and choked with rotting palm fronds. Rusty metal construction rods that had shifted from their crumbling cement housing protruded outward from the steps, like bones exposed from leprous flesh. Insects darted over the water's surface, which remained stubbornly motionless despite the gentle Caribbean breeze. That soft wind never let up, coming and going as if a feeble desktop fan were rotating somewhere just out of sight.

Even Leon, the smiling handyman, gave up on the pool after a day spent attempting to extract the debris or drain the sludge. "Try dat beach, mon," he suggested, waving abstractly toward a mossy green cliff.

Leon could climb trees, scaling branchless coconut palms with his legs—one was lame and twisted—bent like vise grips against the trunk. Once at the top, he collected two or three young green coconuts and slid back down to earth, cracking the nuts open on a cement wall, and encouraging us to drink the slippery white milk. Dad did so eagerly before handing the coconut over to me. I was ill at ease with my father's instant enthusiasm for primitive living, and about putting my mouth on a jagged hole where my father's mouth, and Leon's before his, had been. Mom stayed on the shady patio, her back to us, reading a novel and turning a page every few minutes.

The snapshots I took of Jamaica show a place without shelter: low walls, empty sky. Everyone I photographed clutches something, as if to stay grounded. In one picture, Sarah leans into the camera with her arm around the trunk of a palm tree—my stage direction—while Howard's younger son tries to force his way into the frame. In another, Mom stands stiffly in a black-and-white tank suit in front of overgrown tropical foliage. She had not wanted to go on a trip she considered poorly timed and beyond our reach, but she had developed the habit of acquiescing to my father's decisions. Speaking up or disagreeing with him ignited rages, accusatory silences, or threats. Like a stone smoothed by water, Mom lay low.

A cheerful, sweaty housekeeper and her assistant showed up every morning to fry runny eggs and barbecue goat still on the bone. The helper churned tepid vanilla ice cream in the sandy yard where chickens ran free. Her accent was incomprehensible, but she tried hard to be nice, patting my head before she picked ackee fruit from the tree in the yard. I tasted my plate of yellow cooked ackee and pushed it away, claiming that it smelled like steamy talcum powder.

Sarah and I shared a bedroom in Jamaica. Two of us in one room was not a necessity, since an array of bedrooms circled the tiled living room, but I was unnerved by the alien environment and unmoored without Susie. I was prickly and argumentative. To anything, I responded, "I know." The Cokes here are not made with seawater, even though they taste funny. "I know." You can't name a cat Madonna; it's like naming a dog Jesus. "I know."

"I know" added up to "Leave me alone."

Sarah didn't know everything and didn't care. She was adventurous and played TV tag with the boys in the bright, dry yard.

At five and a half years old, Sarah made elaborate plans to keep herself entertained, unraveling the seams of her stuffed bear's ears just enough to fill the ginger-colored half circles with M&Ms for a snack.

The sun set late in Jamaica. Sarah and I lay on our backs in our twin beds, with little to say. We watched palm trees sway in the sunset, splinters of images glimpsed through the latticed gaps in the concrete blocks that joined our walls to our ceiling. Little lizards stalked the wide cement windowsills, moving in tiny, urgent steps. The animals always sensed our presence once they had traveled halfway across the sill. Stock-still, they lifted their heads and exhaled, some forcing a tomato-colored bubble from a pale-green throat before dashing away into the night.

The ocean in Jamaica entranced me—gray-green and glinting, with a salty, sulfurous smell. It had the same drowsing sense of solitude I had grown accustomed to at home. In Jamaica, I heard buzzing insects and lapping waves, and sometimes muffled talk or the flapping of sandaled feet inside the house.

All of us felt disconnected, floating in a kind of syrupy shock, bumping up against one another before drifting away. Sarah was young, but she surely must have felt our distraction. With Sarah and Mom, the three of us holding hands and leaning back to counterbalance every step, I navigated the concrete steps on the cliffside, heading down to the beach. I waded in the ocean a little bit—I did not yet know how to swim—looking up the cliff at the house and wondering if it was worth the effort to go back up for the towel I had forgotten. Sarah was not allowed to be exposed to seawater past her knees because of the risk of infection. As a unit, we moved toward the water and darted back like hermit crabs, unable to surrender to the ocean.

The adults spent most days at the house, sprawled in patio chairs staring out at the sea. Leon had proven his worth by delivering bags of pot in exchange for cartons of cigarettes, and demonstrating how to roll joints—spliff, in Jamaica—using entire pages of the local telephone book. Dad and Howard savaged the slender directory and asked the housekeeper if she couldn't please bring them her copy. The joints Dad rolled were the size of waffle cones. At home, Dad had a red plastic rolling machine the size of two long fingers, and routinely ground his dope fine in the blender. All adults, as far as I knew, smoked pot.

But in Jamaica, my father's pot smoking irked me. When he was stoned on the patio overlooking the sea, Dad smiled and reached out to pet my hair or called me "Jesserbaby." His gestures were slow. His regression to the attentive Dad he had been before Susie got sick felt false to me, and I withdrew from him.

One afternoon, Howard or Dad organized a one-day expedition into Kingston from Ocho Rios, a distance of less than one hundred miles south down the island. Jamaica's Blue Mountains run like vertebrae in the island's eastern side, protecting a dense rain forest that I had been told was inhabited by cannibals. My mother craved a break from the oversized cockroaches at the house and the windy cliff, but a day free of my father outweighed her desire for a change of scene. She stayed in her chair on the patio with her novel.

I was torn: I wanted to stay and to go. Safe with Mom or on the verge of danger with Dad. If I expressed too strong a desire to stay behind, my father's feelings would be hurt, and I worried that he would tease me for being lazy or afraid.

Kingston was reached by train, one that hauled passengers, mail, and produce one way and the occasional threadbare East Indian businessman toting a cardboard suitcase the other. Goats and chickens occupied the center aisle, falling to the left or right when the train took a curve. Hands in my lap, I kept watch out of the corner of my eye for a cannibal ambush, and calculated how I would escape the bloody fray when it came.

After about an hour on the train, a group of women who had been singing hymns struck up a conversation.

"What songs do you sing in church in the United States?" asked the woman closest to me, leaning forward to speak.

Should I explain that I didn't go to church, and hardly ever to synagogue? I wondered.

Facing a group of black women, the first song that surfaced in my mind was "We Shall Overcome." My father had learned the spiritual from his friends in the civil rights movement and roared it often enough at home. He would overcome someday, and he would live in peace someday. There were days when I couldn't get the tune out of my head, so I devised harmonies or inserted an upbeat "ooh baby" between the phrases "deep in my heart" and "I do believe," just to spice it up.

Were Jamaicans oppressed? I wondered. Did they know who Martin Luther King Jr. had been? Was it even okay for me to sing an African-American protest song? Instead, I mumbled the name of a song I had learned in Girl Scouts, "He's Got the Whole World in His Hands." Sick to my stomach, I stumbled through a demonstration of the first verse, making halfhearted cradling motions at the words "little bitty babies," scooping my arms around my head at the words "whole world." I wished fervently that I could be transported back home to Atlanta, where I would not be impelled to lead strangers in song.

In Kingston I bought a ruby-colored straw tote bag as big as an ottoman, which lasted for decades and spent its final days as a faded laundry bag. I gaped at my first ocean liner, which looked to me like a Manhattan high-rise emerging from the sea.

Jittery and inscrutable behind his shades, my father loped through the markets and pointed out sights faster than I could turn my head to follow. Look, a cargo ship, a wharf rat, a puddle. Look, a slum street veering off from the harbor. Don't stare—you know that makes other people feel small. Look, a man coming toward us, going past us, on a bicycle, a donkey cart, a moped, going away.

8.

Sarah would listen, but she's asleep in the hosp. For
such a little kid, she's so used to hospitals and all.
She's so tough! Smart, too. And beautiful. I'm not
jealous, because I know that I am smart and tough.
Egleston brings back not painful memories, just a
strong feeling of hurt and injustice.

—Journal, November 1973

We left the concrete house and the stony beach and came
back to Atlanta in time for Sarah and me to start the new
school year. My skin had baked to the brown-red color of
anthills, which other kids joked about, as if I'd undergone a
transformation at the beach. The teasing didn't last long,
deflating into a limp trial balloon of a forbidden word.
Eleven-year-olds have short attention spans; they soon
turned their attention to a fluffy-headed dandelion of a girl
who spoke only Greek.

After Susie died, I began collecting details of the lives around me. Inventorying the minutiae of my loved ones' lives would hold them still in my mind, tethering them to the kitchen table, the front seat of the car, or the auditorium during assembly at school. I had been casual in my relationship with Susie, and although I knew I had not been responsible for her illness or her death, both events proved to me that I could no longer allow the world to turn without my fervent attention. I imagined that I had grown a huge eye and an elephantine ear that allowed me to catch the sights and sounds that weaker, less alert individuals missed: which kinds of bread the delivery man unloaded at the grocery store while I held my breath and loitered by the gumball machine, or the number of times a woodpecker rapped on a pine tree outside our family room.

If I could notice everything around me, I would have worked hard enough to keep everyone alive.

Sarah took daily antibiotics to forestall infections. When she was well, she participated fully in daily life, but our parents and Sarah learned not to make long-range plans, in case a hospitalization or serious infection interfered. Sarah might be able to join the field trip to the planetarium or go to a friend's birthday party. Mom signed the permission slips or RSVP'd for the party, just in case, but Sarah knew there were no promises. I never saw her throw a tantrum about it. Her mouth was often sore, a side effect of her pills, and Mom swabbed the inside of Sarah's lips with a medicine called Gentian Violet that smelled to me like dirty socks and made Sarah look as if she had been eating grape candy.

When the first and second graders performed a play commemorating the burning of Atlanta in the Civil War, Sarah got the role of a flame, one of a gang of kids who would turn the city to ash. My mother assembled a costume of orange pants and clutches of bright crepe-paper streamers. With her classmates, Sarah jumped up and down on the periphery of the stage during the climactic scene, shaking her paper flames, screaming, "Atlanta is burning!"

In those years when Susie's death was new, Sarah and I did not talk about our sister, or discuss what we remembered about her. We didn't say that we missed her, or imagine out loud the things she would be doing now if she were alive. I was following my parents' lead by not looking back, trying to protect the two of us from the sorrow that came from imagining things that could not come true.

As early as first grade, Sarah was good with words and good at math, a subject I balked at, unwilling to accept that one-half and two-fourths and four-eighths could amount to the same thing.

"Think of fractions like languages," Mom told me, exasperated. She alighted on a kitchen chair, trying to will me to concentrate on my homework. "*Bonjour* is to *hello* as two-fourths are to one-half. They're different ways to say one thing that has the same meaning."

"Why give the same thing different names?" I whined. "Just call it all the same thing, and leave me out of it."

Things should be whole. Fractions were ominous proof that everywhere, not just in our family, objects break apart and pieces fall away.

Sarah sat across the kitchen table, breezing through her homework, listening to me protest about mine. Her math talent was circumstantial—she had absorbed the logic behind pill dosages and the way meds were calculated for her body weight.

More than a dozen years later, Sarah would excoriate me in a restaurant in New York because I still couldn't figure a tip. "Move the decimal," she said through gritted teeth. My sister was beautifully dressed even in old jeans, a T-shirt, and a designer jacket she'd found at a discount shop. She wore her heavy blonde hair pulled away from her face, hanging down her back. She looked at me, hard. "Round the number up or down to the nearest multiple of ten and then move the damned decimal to the left!"

I couldn't do it, break some invisible mental rule and allow myself to move numbers around in a way that seemed dangerously willy-nilly. Sarah determined the tip, not much on two bowls of seafood bisque, salads, and iced tea. By the time we left the restaurant, we were laughing—our big sister and little sister roles reversed again.

∴

When Sarah was small, her medications were changed often: physicians' calculations resulting in stronger and stronger dosages of antibiotics that we called horse pills, big, smelly ovals that she was able to swallow without water.

In those days, my parents' bedroom was divided land. Dad put a chain lock on the inside of the door, not to protect their privacy but to shut everyone out, including my mother. He made a magpie's nest of their bed: an ocean-sized California king mattress for which he had the wooden frame specially made. He claimed a bad back, digestive trouble, or a headache. Often, he alternated between depression and manic fire, a misery that I knew even then was poorly treated with amphetamines, barbiturates, marijuana, and Scotch.

Seduced by my father's charisma, his doctors and therapists had become his friends and accomplices. Some wrote advances on his prescriptions, giving him license for two to three months' worth of pills at a time, and he gave clusters of the white slips of paper to his pharmacist. On the days Dad lay in bed, Mom drove to the drugstore before it opened, waving at the pharmacist through the glass door, handing over Dad's prescription refills once the druggist let her in. Mom had started part-time work as a secretary at a university law journal, to earn extra money. If Jack is quiet, she thought, I can get out of the house and go to work. If Jack stays out of our way, Sarah can go to a friend's house after school, and Jessica can go to the library and study.

Some days he slept all morning and spent his afternoons in bed, watching television and smoking cigarettes. He had gone into private practice with another lawyer in a small downtown firm. When Sarah and I heard the chain lock scrape against his bedroom door, we sat immobile. Dad drifted into the kitchen in his underwear. Sometimes he would pat our heads, flat-handed, as if we were dangerous dogs. Other days he staggered back to his room without seeing us, trailing saltine crackers or gnawing a salami. I tried not to breathe, afraid that if he saw me, I would be found culpable of some random transgression.

My father was frightened by his daughters' illnesses. He had lost one child, and had another who was fatally ill. He was worried about money, because medical costs were unpredictable and his law firm was new. Sometimes, to keep himself going, he took speed. Because amphetamines keep the user awake, they can offer twenty-four useful hours in a day. I see now that this must have been a kind of freedom for my father: a chance to be superhuman. More time for hospital visits, hounding doctors, paying bills, and working, but in his battle to conquer time, my father had gotten aggressive and paranoid.

In those years, my parents worked hard to maintain family life. Their style had never been one of physical affection with each other in front of their children, and I didn't miss not seeing them kiss or hold hands. My parents pretended our lives were normal.

Sarah and I spent some weekend afternoons with Mom at her parents' house, in a neighborhood a few miles away. (Soon after Susie was diagnosed, my grandfather took early retirement from his draftsman's job with Bethlehem Steel, sold his home south of Boston, and moved to Atlanta.)

On one of these afternoons, while Mom drove us home from her parents' house, Sarah and I squabbled in the car, and I twisted around from the front seat to grab at her. Any chance to live a normal life pointed to Mom's true North, and she let us argue, drowning us out with the classical station on the car radio.

The closer we came to our house, the more apprehensive I felt. I'm sure that my mother shared my dread—she cherished her days with her parents. Accelerating hard to bring her car up our steep driveway, Mom ruptured the membrane that separated the outside world from home. We soared past the persimmon tree on our left and the camellia bushes on our right, hoping that my father was out and we would be the first ones home. When Mom stopped the car and pulled on her hand brake, we saw Dad's red sedan parked behind the house, under the rotting basketball hoop. Out of habit, the three of us kept quiet, and formed a wedge, big, medium, and small, before entering the house.

Cabinet doors hung open in the kitchen, and stray pieces of food littered the countertop. Glasses and plates teetered in the sink.

"Jack?" my mother called softly. (For a period of several months he tolerated no loud noises. Laughing or shouting hurt his ears, or his head, or broke his heart.)

She tapped on their bedroom door, waiting for him to release the lock. I felt something dark coming like a whirlwind, and busied myself with an invented task in my room. I opened my bedroom door the slightest crack to see my father hopping from one foot to the other while he pulled on his pants as he moved toward the back door.

"That's what I think of your father!" he bellowed over his shoulder.

After my father's car had roared away, Mom, tense and silent, busied herself with getting dinner ready. When we came to the table, we talked about school, our afternoon with our grandparents, about anything but what had just happened.

Before dinner, I tiptoed into my parents' empty bedroom. Magnetized by the horror and the energy in that room, I spent hours there when no one was home, poking with my toe at clothes piled on the floor, picking up books and putting them down again, tasting dead cigarettes. Alone in their room, I could sit in the depression left by my father's weight in the white sheets of the unmade bed and stare at the view of the backyard. This is what the tulip poplar looks like if you're Dad, I thought. This is what the pine straw looks like if you're Mom.

On that afternoon, Dad scrawled *Scum-Sucking PIG!* in letters the size of my hand on their bedroom wall. What he wrote made less of an impression on me than the unruly act of his putting pencil to plaster.

"Shape up!" Mom screamed at Dad when he stormed home. In her heart, my mother knew that her husband had mentally come apart, but she believed herself unable to take care of Sarah and me alone. Mom was not willing to have a third member of her family sick, or watch an adult behave like a child. She could not allow my father to break.

I don't know if a specific event caused my father's outburst that day, but it became increasingly clear after Susie died that he wanted to close a circle around us and keep much of the outside world away.

I never saw my father weep after Susie's death. Sarah's hospitalizations were not explained to me beyond the basic information that would tell me what she was "in for"—we used jailhouse slang as comic relief, alleviating our tension—and when she was expected to come home. I didn't usually ask. Dad was a man under pressure, and I think by then he could see no way out.

In college, Mom and Dad had taken a humanities class together. They studied a variety of things, including the ancient Jewish maxims called the "Ethics of the Fathers"—the "Pirkei Avot." My mother became enamored of the belief expressed there that "if I am only for myself, what am I?" When she was small, her own father, rather than the Hebrew sages, reminded her about the Golden Rule. She wanted to see these principles instilled in me. Rather than quoting lines of text with only abstract meaning, she sent me with my father on his good works, trusting that I would learn the concepts firsthand.

Dad's moods were erratic after Susie's death. Sometimes he asked me to come with him like old times. Sometimes I went to appease him. We had all changed. My mother's focus and routine now tugged at me as strongly as my father's constant motion had before. My internal compass pointed away from my father and toward my quiet and strong mother. Like Mom, I began to deal with my losses silently. I did not argue with Dad or make my deepest feelings known. If I did, Dad would sometimes tell me that I was oversensitive or selfish.

My father loved all words. He had dreamed of being an English professor, but because his father expected him to join his law practice, or because his parents would pay for law school but not an advanced degree in literature, or because a particular undergrad professor didn't like him (his answer depended on when you asked), he did what was expected of him and became a lawyer. As a grown man, he spoke to everyone as if they were capable of caressing language with his same fervor. He often spoke in intricate sentences, with a rolling, anaphoric rhythm. He did not appear to be showing off; he was simply sharing the wealth. If you didn't know what he meant, it was your obligation to look it up. Later, looking words up in the big gray dictionary on the desk in the family room became a game for Sarah and me: know a word before Dad uses it.

He recited long passages of poetry without being prompted. For Chanukah, 1969, he gave me a collection of what was then called Negro poetry. My father read to me from "I Am the Darker Brother" before I went to bed; "We Real Cool," the tempo gaining as he spoke; or "Incident," which started out like a nursery rhyme and ended with such hurt feelings.

When we left the house together, him driving me to school or on an errand or as his companion at one of his friends' homes, he held open the back door and intoned, "Let us go, then, you and I."

Pulling on my coat if it were winter, or sliding my feet into sandals most of the year, I replied, "Yes, let's," presuming that Dad was making a formal statement. He kept going, gathering tumbling words, his voice made deeper by their sounds. The part about the patient etherized upon the table confused me, but I didn't ask what he meant. I assumed he was making an indirect reference to Susie or Sarah. My father was somewhere in his head, and my job was to listen and learn.

For the first year or two after we came back from Jamaica, I followed my parents' instructions and came directly home from school to start dinner, with groceries bought by Mom on Saturday and the directions left for me every day in her neat, bristly handwriting. She had moved on from her secretarial job to work as a court reporter. Her schedule changed nearly every day, and she welcomed the adventure of driving deep into the country to an old-fashioned courtroom.

My mother sat in a front corner inside rural county courthouses, antique brick buildings in the center of languid town squares where farmers congregated in the shadow of the clock tower to sell strawberries and collard greens from their truck beds. In court, the judge and attorneys greeted my mother by name. She repeated every word of a trial into a reel-to-reel tape recorder, speaking softly into a microphone buried in a gray plastic cone.

At home, she demonstrated the apparatus for Sarah and me, holding the cone like a mask over her nose and mouth, laughing and swinging her head from side to side and trumpeting like an elephant. My mother still did not always understand the thickest southern accents. She would listen to the tapes time and time again until she deciphered the words that sounded to her like a dream played back in slow motion.

The money she earned from court reporting was turned over to Dad. He wrote the checks, he paid the bills, and my mother believed that he was still in charge.

While I cooked in the afternoons, I waited for my mother's father to bring Sarah home. He picked her up from school—her day was done before mine—and with our grandmother kept her entertained at their house. He plied Sarah with old-fashioned Jewish food that she liked but I called gross: bowls of cold purple borscht from the Manischewitz jar, served with a floating orb of sour cream on top, or beige loaves of damp gefilte fish on small plates. At least once, our grandfather took Sarah to the hospital. Usually, though, he brought Sarah home by four and dropped her off with me, catching my attention by tooting his car horn at the crest of our driveway.

He and I knew better than to offer or accept an invitation into our house. To do so would get me in trouble with Dad, and would hurt my grandfather's feelings by asking something of him he could not do.

Instead, my grandfather idled his maroon Mercury in the driveway, reaching across the passenger seat to lift the door handle and let little blonde Sarah out. He waited to see that she got safely into the house. I waved to him from the back door, or walked out to talk to him, leaning in to the driver's side window of his car and smelling the cherry odor of his tobacco.

When Susie was living, and for a brief time after her death, my grandparents did come to our house, my grandfa-

ther smoking his pipe in our family room and restlessly leafing through magazines, my grandmother helping my mother
in the kitchen, or indulging her granddaughters' play with
stuffed animals and troll dolls.

My father's irritation at his in-laws was a storm that
gathered before it burst. He may have believed that my
mother told elaborate stories to her parents about his anger,
his drug use, the ways he had begun to fail us. He was not
close to his own parents, and must have been uncomfortable with my mother's love for hers.

But Mom kept the truth about the distance in her marriage and my father's black moods from her parents. Accustomed to cultivating a sterile environment for Susie and
Sarah, she created another kind for her parents. Jack is working, she lied. Jack is out of town on business. Jack is fine.

My grandfather Eli believed that a man held a job and
earned a living, especially if his children were not well. Dis-
turbed by the rumors of daytime sleeping and by the tension he sensed in his daughter, my grandfather confronted
my father on a day when all of us were home. "You're running with the Shebas," my grandfather accused.

"You're a son of a bitch!" my father bellowed.

Quarreling with his father-in-law, my father's face
flushed. He raked his hands through his hair. During the
past few months, he had begun to let it hang oily and limp.
My grandfather shouted back. He was taller than my father
by an inch or two. My father was a tree, but my grandfather
was a mountain. From where I stood, watching through the

windows in the family room, I could not hear my father's voice, but I could guess how he sounded. When he was angry, his voice flattened to a terrifying monotone.

I saw my grandfather, in the yard, bend toward my father and wag his finger as he replied. I could tell from his posture that he was yelling. He got into his car, and backed down the driveway, sliding out of sight between the pine trees.

"You had better never come back!" my father howled.

· · ·

When I was very small and until I was nine or ten, we girls were the future. As the first child, I was the one my father felt closest to and the one to whom he offered his legacy. Very late one night in April 1968, my father woke me, hours before my mother would rouse me for breakfast. Susie slept undisturbed in the bed on the other side of the window, even though my father had switched on the bedroom light. He sat on my bed, close to the pillow. He smelled of cigarettes. He had been away all day, past dinner, which was not uncommon. Under his arm, he had a shiny white cardboard sign, the kind I knew people carried on protest marches. The sign had been bent in half, as if at the waist, to fit in his suitcase on the plane.

My father unfolded the cardboard sign and held it upright. "Honor King, End Racism" was printed on it in bold, black lettering. Dad had been on a march.

"I carried this in Memphis today," he said. "I'm giving it to you."

In many ways, I think that I failed my father. I was clumsy, unable to sail basketballs from a pretend half-court in the backyard. I did not want to save the world, and I found Bob Dylan's and Joan Baez's singing boring and pious. As Susie and Sarah got sicker, I failed him because I fell silent. I did not cry, or cling to him, or tell him my troubles. When asked why I couldn't be civil or answer a question, I shrugged in reply. By the time I was ready to talk, my father was too unstable to trust.

One night he made kindling of a wooden mask my maternal grandfather made, dropping it into the blazing fireplace. Mom stood in the doorway and screamed; Dad cursed at her in return. I watched from the adjacent dining room for only a minute before I tiptoed away, wishing I could erase the scene. On other nights my father sat withdrawn and empty-eyed. After Susie died, there was rare reward or comfort in turning to him.

To a degree, I believe that my father was angry with me for having a future. Always a dramatic man, given to excess and great emotion, his intellect was choked by terror and clouded by drugs. Instead of raising a hand, he hurled words. No one cares what you think, he'd tell me if I expressed an opinion about meals or fashion. Only a few years before, he had encouraged my childish attempts to hold up my end of the conversation.

"I'm sorry," I would tell my father, when my footfalls were too loud in the hallway or when I stayed on the phone too long at night.

"Sorry doesn't cut it," he answered. "Sorry is never good enough."

Each on their own paths, my parents felt helpless. The sixties enveloped my father, and every joss stick and soul handshake reminded him how hard he had bucked against conforming to the life his parents' generation had expected of him. After Susie and Sarah got sick, he was more than trapped; he was emasculated. He was able to help strangers, the underpaid textile workers in the mills and the drug addicts and petty criminals in Atlanta, but he was helpless for the people who needed and loved him the most.

. . .

"You only get to make one phone call from jail, and when you do, you want to make sure someone gets your cry for help," Dad said.

He kept a yellow legal pad and a jam jar of clotted ballpoint pens by the kitchen phone. I took a few messages from junkies and pimps making their one call to Dad, a few more from bail bondsmen. "Free at Last" Bail Bond company. Even when I was twelve, the resolute sense of irony in that joke made me wince. I called Dad at work the minute I hung up from these calls: his home and office numbers were listed in the phone book in hopes of his being always available to the needy.

"Jack Handler, please," I said to his secretary.

Dad came on the phone, audibly grinding his teeth from amphetamines and tension. Inevitably, Dad would launch into a quiz that quickly devolved into a harangue.

"Did he say 'Tom' or 'Tim'?"

"Are you sure the last number was two?"

"Was that the Fulton County Jail or the DeKalb County Jail?"

Are you sure are you sure are you sure.

I had nightmares about faceless men and women, always poor, always thin, wasting away in jail because I had inadvertently transposed a telephone number or misspelled a name. The horrible way that a stranger might spend his or her last days would be my fault, because I had overlooked something simple, something that could have been made right.

Trying to impress some sense of danger on me and show me, too, the faces of the victims of the world, Dad took me with him on a visit to the Fulton County Jail. I had become a sullen, stare-down-at-my-feet kind of kid. The jail, as unending and impersonal as a hospital, smelled of disinfectant. I shook hands with a cop, and stayed close to my father, breathing in his familiar scent of tobacco and dry-cleaned Brooks Brothers suit. Every footfall and telephone ring echoed beneath bars of fluorescent lights so harsh that my eyeballs felt peeled.

After Susie died, it seemed as if every time I lifted my head to look at my family, I saw that we had been shaken so hard we had blown apart. We never spoke about Sarah's infections and headaches and hospitalizations, or about Dad's dark moods and elusive rules.

Sound engineers call their method of reducing extraneous noise "baffling." A microphone on location is swaddled

Jack, Sarah, Mimi, Atlanta, 1972

in foam to baffle the whistling wind. A set is draped with heavy cloth to baffle the sounds of traffic outside. Swaddled in bewilderment and fear, I was, in every sense of the word, baffled.

I found small ways to hurt myself in order to feel alive. Tearing out hunks of my hair made my eyes sting, but thrilled me; I felt physical pain, but I made myself keep secret that I was damaging my healthy body. My heart hammering, I buried the hair in a shroud of toilet paper at the bottom of my bathroom trash can.

Rages boiled up inside me without warning. The skin on my forearms and in the small of my back crawled, and my teeth felt as if they itched with the need to bite and draw blood. What I wanted to do was scream, but our family code required silence about dire emotion. Instead, I opened my mouth wide, and learned to scream without making a sound. This made me even angrier, and my field of vision turned milky white, then blank. I knelt on my bedroom floor and banged my forehead on the wood until pain shot through my temples and the room spun. I stopped just short of passing out. When a parent asked about a swollen cheek or a blue bruise that shaded my temple, I shrugged and made excuses.

I felt that my family had been cheated. An eclipse had passed over the five of us. My mother was strained, my father unstable, I felt invisible, Susie was dead, and Sarah was small and pretty, her lips ragged and cracked from infections, teeth stained shingle-gray from antibiotics, with an insistent cough that sounded like marbles shaken in a jar. I was afraid, too, that what I thought of as "it"—the illnesses that shrouded our family in darkness—would come for me. If that happened, then every one of us—Susie, Sarah, my father, and me—would have failed, leaving my mother alone in an empty home.

As a family, we talked about anything but death, turning away from the thing that skirted our lives. Speaking of death was as unthinkable an act as tearing off your clothes at the dinner table or kicking a small animal.

Susie's tightly made empty bed was painful to look at. If we moved the single bed to a different place in the room, I thought, it would no longer be Susie's bed, but could take on the characteristics of a sofa. The idea of bringing the subject up with Mom made me feel weak, but after a few days, I told her my idea. My mother agreed, and made rearranging the room a project for the two of us.

With my mother's help, I moved Susie's bed against the wall and padded it with new throw pillows, making a place for studying and reading in the room that was now only mine. Together, we repainted the walls and bought new purple wicker furniture and a rug shaped like a footprint. We were moving forward. We kept our unhappiness to ourselves.

The day of my twelfth birthday party, my father left his bedroom and walked up the stairs to the attic. He climbed out of the window onto the flat roof over the den, dressed only in his underpants. Standing there like the figurehead on a ship's prow, he peered into the sun, one hand angled at his brow. At the moment my father popped through the attic window, Mom and I were waiting below for a small group of girls attending my party.

I had gotten used to seeing my father wander the house wearing nothing but his white cotton briefs, but standing high above me, his legs looked spindlier, and his chest was so hairless and concave that it shone. My father's stomach protruded, and I knew from his drumming on his skin when he lay in bed that the curve of his belly was hard and hollow sounding, not soft and loose like what my mother insisted was baby fat on my upper arms and hips. I looked up at Dad and down the driveway, right to left, swiveling my head. My stomach soured, and my shoulders rose up around my ears. Which of my friends would show up first to see Dad on top of the house and discover our secret—that we were insane?

"*Oh, Freedom,*" Dad sang. He had a passionate baritone, and the spirituals that had been given new life in the civil rights movement meant the most to him. Swaying as if he were a link in a solidarity chain at a march, he bellowed, "*Before I'd be a slave, I'd be buried in my grave, and go home to my Lord and be free.*"

Mom spun around, looking back at the house and around the yard before her sight moved toward the roof.

"*There'll be singing, there'll be shouting . . . ,*" Dad roared.

In an instant, she screamed, "Get in the house! Please get in the house and please be quiet!" Instead, he sang louder before he switched to cawing like a crow in a call-and-response rhythm to her pleading, tucking his hands into his armpits and flapping his elbows.

My mother called a friend of my father's, who coaxed Dad down from the roof. He took him to lunch and kept him safely away until long after my friends had left and I had gone to bed.

Within another year or so, my father would check into a mental hospital. By then, he could no longer pretend that all was well.

9.

I wanted to get really wrecked so I can't even walk,
but I'm sort of chicken.

—Journal, January 1974

Until eighth grade, the first year of high school in Atlanta in the early 1970s, I mostly flew under the radar. When I did speak up, I was a brain and a priss. I was the kid who could be counted on to have already read the books assigned in English class. The kid who had to go straight home after school to babysit her sister, because her parents both worked. The kid who had a sister who died. I was smart, but I wasn't savvy. When the country-talking boy with hair flat as sandpaper offered me a stick of gum after the dismissal bell rang, I was dumb enough to take it.

At the time, rumors of purple microdot acid smaller than a tab of saccharine and LSD licked from the backs of postage stamps circulated through school. My inaugural acid trip was the kind health science class filmstrips warned about—head trip by Juicy Fruit.

For the half hour before the number 16 bus disgorged me at my stop, I was hypnotized by my reflection in the window. My dark hair and my gapped front teeth were superimposed over the trees and stop signs and landmarks I saw every day. Awestruck by the presence of my window-face looking back at me, I mugged in a bus-window movie where I could look right through my own face onto the street. Me as part of my landscape. My movie-hand came up to my movie-jaw, where my movie-mouth hung slack. In the window, I watched my movie-fingers wiggle into my movie-mouth. Finally, I thought, it has come for me—I am really, incontrovertibly, sick. I curled up like a cocktail shrimp on the hard bus seat and started to cry.

When the bus stopped, two friends from elementary school who had figured out what was happening grabbed my elbows and steered me out the door and onto the curb. They hot-walked me like a racehorse into the drugstore, stashing me indoors until they could figure out what to do with me.

Jane and Mary Beth bought Cokes and gossip magazines at the counter and prepared to wait me out. I lay on the floor and began to sing a rock hit about a bullfrog. While I sang, I twirled the greeting card spinner until it reached warp speed.

When I eventually began to come down, Jane and Mary Beth walked with me until their streets crossed North Highland Avenue, where they pointed me in the direction of home. I walked past brick houses with neat lawns bordered by azaleas, camellias, and pine trees, a route of less than a mile that I had traveled almost every day since first grade. When I emerged from my bedroom for dinner that night, I stayed quiet. While I ate, I thought about how in one afternoon I had gone crazy and come back looking just the same.

The summer after eighth grade, some cool kid in a generous moment decided that I could be cool, too. And there I was, bestowed with a membership in a tribe, leaning against the brick wall behind the minimart, slumping in an oversized army jacket with pockets deep enough to hide heavy bottles of stolen sweet wine. There I was, walking barefoot in empty neighborhood streets after dark, one of a half-dozen teenagers trekking the asphalt center line, oozing like ectoplasm from home to home.

City planners had emptied sections of our neighborhood to make room for a highway that never came through. In abandoned living rooms and fly-specked, waterless kitchens, my friends and I played our own version of "house," breaking and entering into deserted homes where we could do as we pleased.

Sitting in the sun on backyard decks depleted of hibachis, we decorated our cigarettes with black stripes of rank, gummy THC that went undetected by our parents and teachers. We lounged in pine-paneled family rooms empty of furniture, and feasted on chocolate cake frosting direct from the can and bags of Fritos, washing our meals down with Coca-Cola Slurpees from the minimart. When the novelty of independence wore off around twilight, we moved on to our own homes to drink sweet tea and eat globs of peanut butter scooped in soup spoons. We paired off in bedrooms papered with Black-Lite posters and later got up again, disheveled, to drift to the next home, refrigerator, or bedroom.

When I could get into my parents' room, I sorted the cash and pills on my father's bureau into slack pyramids. The tens and twenties I moved to my wallet, snug in the left front pocket of my jeans. The pills I sold for two dollars each, passing them through my opened bedroom window after my parents had gone to sleep. Speed and downers went out, and dollar bills came in. If my father noticed his stash diminishing or his pocket money running low, he didn't say. I never stole Sarah's drugs. Antibiotics have no entertainment value, and her medicine was, in its way, sacred.

Pot and pills seemed to be everywhere then, as constant as music from car radios.

Pot did lead to the harder stuff, at least among the heads in inner-city public high school and the dropouts who waited in their cars for the three o'clock bell to launch the daily party. After a while the harder stuff and the softer stuff mixed together. One big happy family. The days I was free of babysitting (Sarah sick and in the hospital, Sarah well and gone for dinner and a sleepover at a friend's house) were afternoons and evenings of bottomless thrill. Pile into someone's brother's Dodge Dart with the empty beer cans rolling on the floor and end up at someone else's cousin's boyfriend's apartment. Wander poolside to find a few bare-chested guys leaning shoulder deep into black garbage bags, sorting kilo bricks of sticky green pot.

Mesmerized by power and divided by my own responsibilities, I became my own conflicted twin. I hurried home from school on the days I was needed, nervous that all my hanging out would get me there too late to save Sarah from some disaster.

At home, Sarah and I usually ignored each other. We relished the chance to push away like oppositional magnetic poles, like a regular teenager and little sister. When Sarah was well, she would have been happy for me to stay away and leave her to her own devices: television, a snack, an hour to practice the piano before walking to a friend's house up the street. When she was sick, she stayed in the hospital and I was on my own, guilty at being empty-handed, temporarily released from sister surveillance and protection. Without her, much of the time I felt lost.

But when Sarah was home, I wanted to be free of her, to let loose and play bumper pool at the recreation center beside the elementary school, to feel the pulse of throbbing bass and keening guitars from the stereo, and to smoke pot in homemade pipes.

While I chopped onions and marinated meat, Sarah would change into a sweatshirt and old jeans, exchange her sneakers for soft leather moccasins, play with the cats, and make herself a snack of cheese and crackers before she settled into a chair at the kitchen table. Once there, she simultaneously turned on the television and strapped the nebulizer tube over her nose and mouth. Miles away, Mom murmured the accusations and defenses of strangers into a plastic mask. At home, Sarah inhaled antibiotic mist through a mask of her own. She coughed hard enough to make me wince, but she stayed sitting upright, as if the racking sound came from somewhere else. Her eyes never left *Sesame Street*. The aqua-blue nebulizer looked like a kitchen appliance and hummed like a generator. The waxy smell of the medicine mixed with the scent of bay leaf and onions from the stove. When I was done, I sat with Sarah while she did her homework.

When the phone rang, I dove for it, hoping it was a friend calling from the minimart, the neighborhood delinquent's center of the earth. At least once an afternoon, Mom called from work, making sure we were home safely, that we had gotten a snack, and were doing our homework.

At least three times in an afternoon, Dad would call to ask what had come in the mail, to ask if anything else had come in the mail that we had neglected to mention, and once more to have Sarah or me carefully open and read all the mail to him.

"Nothing yet, Dad," I answered. Or, "Sarah's gone down the hill to get the mail. Do you want to wait?" He didn't.

When Sarah came in the back door, she carried bills from hospitals, insurance companies, and pharmacies. She stopped to pet the cat before she tossed the mail on the table. Sarah was eight or nine years old then. The contents of the mail must have made her disgusted and embarrassed.

Many of these bills came because of her. Hospitals. Insurance companies. Doctor This and Doctor That.

We could throw away the circulars from the Big Apple market, but not until we had shaken them to make sure no correspondence had stuck in the pages. What else was in the mail? A birthday party invitation for Sarah, a card from Grandma, the new issue of *Commentary*.

"Are you sure that's it?" Dad asked. "Are you absolutely certain?"

I never knew what he was expecting, but every day that we opened the mail and he was dissatisfied with what we had, I wanted to cry.

I was envious of Sarah. She was the focus of our parents' attention, although the reason for their preoccupation was clear. They counted her pills, added new names to her list of doctors, and glanced at her hands to see if a ragged cuticle or an insect bite had turned angry overnight.

Sarah didn't particularly want to be Sarah. She lived a double life; sometimes she was the sick girl, sometimes the well one. She wanted one identity, free of inspection. She was envious of me.

For my sophomore year, I transferred to an innovative private school then a few years old, on an old street where professors and doctors grew big gardens and tied bandannas around the necks of their Irish setters.

My father resisted the move. Attending public school was my social responsibility, a guarantee that I would never lose my empathy for the rank and file. Public school, I complained, was where my English teacher told a room of dozing teenagers that *A Midsummer Night's Dream* was written by a man named "Shacks-pee-yaree." When my father told me that private school was elitist, Mom took my side, and won out. Fulfilling my social responsibility had gotten me failing grades and a habit of skipping school with my friends to shoplift nail polish from the drugstore.

Mom grew up in a home where sacrifice in pursuit of education was made without question. She assumed she would raise her own children the same way: innocent of trouble, elevated by love. I was the child whom fate had determined would be most able to fulfill her own inherent promise. I was proxy for Susie and Sarah. Mom perceived Dad as willing to sacrifice my potential in the service of social welfare. Although in theory she shared his commitment to the rank and file, the peril in her own family had changed Mom's ideas about the meaning of greater good.

Some of my new classmates were kids who viewed themselves as homeless in their own homes, children of grim divorces or parents in public life. Although the school was not intended to be a territory for distressed teenagers, we recognized ourselves in one another.

One afternoon at school I took a break in our smoking lounge. Barefoot and happy, I traded jokes with my friend Brian, a tall boy with waist-length hair. I lay on the floor, my chin on my crossed forearms, while he strummed a guitar. Guitars and wooden flutes stood sentry around the lounge, a sunporch furnished with discarded armchairs and sack-bottomed ashtrays, abandoned jackets, and army-surplus backpacks that hadn't made it into class.

"What's this?" interrupted a combative boy who in my worst moments I thought of as Templeton the Rat. He leaned against the wall and narrowed his eyes. Watching his tight smile, I knew that he was planning something devious. Brian knew it, too, and made a frantic slashing gesture across his Adam's apple. Don't do it. I know what you're going to do, and don't do it.

The instigator ignored him. "So what is it that's going on here?" he drawled. "Would it be a case of sibling rivalry?"

The lounge went silent. Everyone, it seemed, was in on a secret I didn't know. A secret about me. The room emptied. My friend took my arm and dragged me out to the fire escape. More privacy out here, he said.

"Your dad wasn't home for a while, was he?" he asked.

Those days my father was rarely home at night or on weekends. As a result, Mom had been exceptionally happy despite herself, talkative and full of plans. Her cheer buoyed Sarah and me. The three of us kidded around, feeling safe and solid.

Brian lit a cigarette and looked out across the tree-lined path that led the few yards to the main building.

"How do you know that?" I asked, following his gaze. I didn't want to look at him. At that moment, he knew more about me than I did.

"Jack was staying at my house. I'm really sorry. I didn't know if you knew, and then I realized you didn't." He

Jessica, high school, 1976

looked closely at me. "Are you cool? If our parents got married, then we would be like brother and sister."

It was weak consolation, but I took the peace offering. I imagined, though, that my father liked him better than he did his daughters. My father had been staying in his house. That sandwich bag of pot this boy passed around in the park at lunch, the flap sealed with spit, might have been my father's.

My father, by this time, had left private practice and turned to managing a drug treatment center, an alternative sentencing program where the strung out were addressed meaningfully as members of "the family."

The treatment center was filled with woozy light. The windows, tall and leaded, casement and stained glass, were caked with dust, and the hallways were cool and dark and smelled alternately of incense, disinfectant, and body odor. The weeds in the lawn grew around red-clay bald spots. The houses that surrounded it began life as tall, deep-porched homes built for large families. Now tilted and chipped, they lived on as Day-Glo-painted head shops and crash pads for teenage runaways.

Dad got up in the middle of the night to fetch an angry runaway boy over in Alabama. Dad went before a judge and kept someone else from going to jail, more than once. Again, Dad was amazing, supreme, and confident. He was nearly trustworthy, in short bursts. He joked at home that our cats were secret agents of the yard, trench-coated employees of the "We Never Sleep Cat Company." Dad told Sarah stories about a made-up boy with iron ankles, and he took me to the movies. My father was trying to show me something about bravery and love, and for a moment, I understood.

At the drug treatment center, Sarah was a beaming flower girl at the wedding of two "family members" who had gotten clean, and adults talked to me about God and Gandhi and Cat Stevens, about love and brotherhood and their struggles with the devils of addiction and loss. They loved my father. They said he helped save their lives. We attended emotional "graduations" where Dad, in a three-piece suit, welcomed his old friend the mayor to the podium.

The day that a member of "the family" threatened his real family, Dad telephoned Mom. Get out of the house now, he ordered. The three of us went to a motel, and the "family" member stalked our front yard until my father coaxed him away. I imagined our assailant wearing a black leather vest and motorcycle boots, chaps over his jeans, waving a pistol in the air, coming down from heroin and speed, screaming a ribbon of syllables and crazed yelps.

In 1976, the center closed for lack of funding. My father tried to raise money to keep the house alive, but none was forthcoming, and he was out of a job. Sarah and I rooted for him. He shimmered with valiant desperation. After the center closed for good, Dad took day trips to other cities for job offers that didn't pan out. They were too short term, not a good use of his skills, or otherwise not right. I believed him. Sarah and I wanted him happy, for his own sake.

Through a family friend, Dad got a job in Pennsylvania, where he had started his career. Mom and Sarah would go with him, but whether to uproot me wasn't entirely clear.

"She shouldn't have to change schools her senior year," my mother insisted. Mom had been contributing money for my tuition, working as a secretary for a group of lawyers she met while court reporting.

By arranging for me to stay in Atlanta, my mother was putting me in a kind of quarantine, safety-sealing me from the danger in my own family.

Mom felt that she was abandoning me, although she did not tell me then. She convinced herself that this arrangement made the most sense: I was doing well in school, and she had found a safe place for me to live. Without my family around me, she believed that I would thrive. I did not tell my parents that I wanted to go with them; I did not recognize that then.

I don't remember a "For Sale" sign in our yard or a real estate agent toting up attributes in a notebook. I was gone by then, all my energy and teenage heart devoted to making a life with my friends. I do not remember saying good-bye to Sarah.

In my journal, I wrote, "A Treatise for 1976 and 1977" in block letters. "I have perhaps unwittingly faced myself with an incomparable challenge. . . . I am, through aggressiveness, social-ness, separation and thought, learning what I can be."

Mom took Sarah and me out for an elegant dinner for my seventeenth birthday. "I believe in ending things with class," Mom said, opening her menu. Sarah, then eleven, ordered a lobster. I told my mother that we weren't ending, only separating. This is good practice for college, I reminded her. I will not make a mess of anyone's plans.

Dad had gone ahead to Pennsylvania, and sent seventeen American Beauty roses down for my birthday. Mom gave me a typewriter. A week later, she and my sister left, too.

My parents anchored me to school and an au pair job. I began to ignore my child-care responsibilities shortly after moving into my employer's home, decamping periodically for the mattresses-on-the-floor apartment of two school friends who had begun, like me, to live prematurely on their own.

When I was small and my sisters' illnesses were new to us, I saw that operating at high pitch was how everything had to be done. With my family far away, I tore through my last year of high school. Toward the end of the school year, I moved to an apartment in my old neighborhood, when the tenant, a friend of my parents', moved in with her boyfriend. I wrote essays for school about sugar colonies in Barbados, about Walt Whitman, Huck Finn, and Sacco and Vanzetti. I played a sheep in a school play, and helped write bylaws for the student steering committee. I wrote notes to myself in the margins of my American Civ notebook, reminders to "Do laundry" and "Buy typing paper!" I went to wild parties nearly every weekend, in apartments, in the park, in bars where no one seemed to care that the kids carousing at the corner table were sixteen and seventeen years old.

There were fourteen students in my graduating class. Mom and Sarah and my grandmother came to Atlanta for my graduation, but my father did not come. He explained that he had dental work scheduled for that day.

I thought at the time he was mad at me for acting against his will and going to private school, and for my part in breaking up what family unit was left by staying in Atlanta. A letter from my mother explained, under the head-

ing "Why Dad Is Not Coming to Graduation: My Views,"
that my father needed a "worry-free" vacation by himself in
Europe. "The time has come," she wrote. "The passport
and tickets are on his dresser, Sarah is not in the hospital,
and we can (just) afford it." She assured me that my father
was interested in my graduation and included her credit
card number so that I could buy a dress for the occasion.

During my senior year I called my parents often, to talk
to Mom and Sarah and sometimes my father. It was rare to
hear his voice, because he was at work, at a party, at a conference. Sometimes I needed more money in my checking
account. I spent my allowance on tickets to a Neil Young
concert, and then needed to get my typewriter fixed. I
couldn't find my glasses and might need another pair. I used
my lunch money to buy beer or tequila at liquor stores
where teenagers weren't carded, and made excuses to my
parents. I was lonely for my family, but was only beginning
to admit it to myself.

When my father did call, I was elated. In my journal, I
reminded myself to tell him, next time, that I remembered
the stories he once told me about Charlemagne the unicorn. I was seventeen, and I missed being a child, with my
parents in charge.

When I talked with Sarah on the phone, her clarity, as
an eleven-year-old, helped ground me.

"Did you know that people come in three categories?"
Sarah asked. "They are either horses, birds, or muffins."

"What kind of categories are those?" I said. "They don't
match."

"Dad is a horse," Sarah answered, determined. "He is forceful, especially when he deals with medicine."

"What about muffins?"

"Muffins are inconsequential. They are soft."

"So, what am I?"

"You are a bird," Sarah said. "Birds are quick and clever. They are creative and pretty."

My sister saw me, even when I couldn't.

part two

· ·.

Family, 1975

10.

You have all the earmarks—I love that word—of
a winner.

—Postcard from my mother, October 1983

Mom bought a tweed blazer for me to wear in college; tailored all over, tucked just a little bit at the waist. I could see how well made it was, and how costly. I tried to wear it, but I could not raise my arms above my head or swing them freely at my sides. I could not take a breath deep enough to feel my ribs expand in my back.

But you look so elegant, my mother said.

It's tight, I whined. I can't move my arms.

She bought me turtleneck sweaters in black, navy, and cranberry-colored wool. When I wore them, my neck itched. Perspiration pooled in my armpits.

But you look so nice, Mom said.

Instead of trim jackets and turtlenecks, I wore pilled and battered old-man-style V-neck pullovers. Why are you hiding yourself? my mother asked. You're dressed like a bag lady.

Sarah and Mom had an easy sense of style, a natural extension of the innate pleasure they each had with their appearance. They liked to lay their clothing out the night before, to buff their nails, to brush their hair with expensive brushes. I preferred to roll into the first thing that I'd left on the floor the night before, and to run a brush once through my hair—a look that created anonymity. Sarah convinced me to sit still while she stood behind my back, so she could twist my thick hair into a French braid. I fidgeted, but in the end, I admired how sophisticated and tidy my hair looked. As a result, Sarah taught me to braid it myself by feel, without using a mirror.

During the summer of 1977 Dad brought me to Boston on a quick tour of the city where he and Mom had spent their college years. He took me to Locke-Ober for oysters and lobster, and to Harvard's Museum of Natural History to see the glass flowers, which I viewed as weird and crumpled Victorian anachronisms. I acted badly and knew it. If it had been up to me, I would have slept all day in the hotel.

Before the start of my freshman year, I worked as a waitress in the coffee shop beside the train station in Harrisburg. At the end of my shifts, I changed out of my white polyester uniform into regular clothes, but I could never shake the smell of grease and ashtrays. When Mom and Sarah picked me up at the end of my shifts, my hair felt stiff from kitchen odor. Sarah had learned to cook, and made spaghetti with clam sauce. After dinner, Sarah and I played backgammon and made up nonsense lyrics to pop songs. She educated me about the different tropical fish in her tank. Late at night, her cat leaped on the piano and ran down the keys, startling everyone awake, but we rarely remembered to put the keyboard cover down.

When school started in the fall, I headed to Boston. I took a cab from the train station to my dorm. While the driver pulled my footlocker out of the car, I glowered at the families whose station wagons and sedans jammed Bay State Road. I projected disdain, but I was inwardly awed at the sight of kids my age being helped into the next stage of their lives by fathers lifting cardboard boxes and mothers carrying armloads of clothing.

My freshman roommate confessed to me, after we became friends, that at first I had frightened her.

"I thought you were an Indian," she said. Cherokee, or maybe Seminole. I had told her I was from Georgia.

Sitting on my bed that first afternoon, wearing my high school attire of a T-shirt and overalls above unshod dirty feet, my hair in a braid down my back, I was a foreign entity to my Manhattan roommate.

I auditioned new handwriting styles on the pages of my journals, writing in minuscule printing from one margin to another, in spirals, or sentences running top to bottom rather than left to right. In class and in the dorm, I fidgeted and couldn't stay still. My "to do" lists, a welcome anchor taught to me in my senior year of high school, unraveled in college as I bounced from one enthusiasm to the next. For a while, it was midnight movies in costume, then volunteering at the college radio station, or trying out new places to hear blues, rock, or reggae. My schoolwork flagged. I knew that my grade point average was sinking, but devouring new experiences meant more to me than studying. Other than a few journalism courses and a class about different philosophical approaches to death, schoolwork seemed flagrantly irrelevant to learning who I was.

At night in our dorm room, and later in our off-campus railroad apartment with linoleum that curled up from the floors like hoary toenails, I carried our telephone into bed with me or sat in the dark bedroom closet with the door shut. Several nights a week I cradled the phone in my lap and dialed. Until I could find the numbers by touch, I turned the rotary dial under the illumination of streetlamp or flashlight. I pushed the numbers for Atlanta directory assistance around the circle, letting the mechanical resistance that followed each push drag my finger back. On these nights, I asked a southern telephone operator for fictional names, then for numbers I already knew by heart. Her voice reminded me of home.

My friends called me boisterous. At a dorm-room party, a girl pierced my left earlobe with a sewing needle and an ice cube after I chose which side would look more rebellious. My part-time job washing dishes in the dining hall meant that I excused myself from the table after dinner to don my apron, hairnet, and elbow-length rubber gloves.

While I brandished an industrial sprayer at the end of a dish-laden conveyor belt, my friends placed messages in the remains of their meals and sent them in to me in the steamy kitchen. "We love you, Jessica," came in on a paper napkin floating atop a bowl of partially eaten ice cream. A design made of raisins pressed into mashed potatoes slid in on a tray. A new crowd had taken me in and made me their own.

In college, I began to struggle with my weight, which hadn't troubled me since puberty. While other students studied and drank coffee or soda, I doodled and licked globs of milkshake from the tip of a straw. When my roommate got a cake as a gift from her mother, she put it on a plate in our dorm room and left to take a shower. While she was gone, I allowed myself to pick off a tiny taste from the back, so small that I told myself no one would notice. I demolished half of the cake pinch by pinch, but only when my roommate came back and I saw her crestfallen look did I realize what I had done.

When I went home during a break my freshman year, my mother said she hadn't recognized me at the airport. Appalled, she put me on a diet mostly of salads, and made me promise to sign up for a weight-loss program when I got back to school. My jeans wouldn't button, and even floppy shirts gapped across my chest and stomach.

I knew I stood on the precipice of a frightening choice. I could be the person I thought my family expected me to be, or I could turn and run. Even losing weight and looking good, I told myself, wouldn't make me a person who could fix anyone's problems.

My junior year, my parents phoned me from Pennsylvania. Dad was in the bedroom upstairs, I knew, and Mom was downstairs, in the kitchen.

When Dad told me he had accepted a job in Indonesia, he sounded like he had when he was in charge of the drug treatment center. An unexpected wave had lifted Dad again.

Hundreds of thousands of Vietnamese refugees had been flooding into Southeast Asian resettlement camps in the years since the end of the Vietnam War. My father was packing his bags to move around the world to direct a refugee services agency in Singapore. Sitting on the floor in my hallway in Boston, I looked at my roommate's backpack and the stack of recycling in the kitchen and wondered where exactly Singapore was. Far, far away. I closed my eyes and leaned my back against the wall, listening on the long-distance line.

"So, I'll be leaving right away," Dad finished. He sounded relieved. "I'll get off the phone now, and let you speak to your mother."

When the upstairs extension clicked off and the echo between their two phones subsided, Mom spoke up. She told me that Dad had always wanted to see Asia.

"You're not going, are you?" I asked. I gripped the curly phone cord like a lifeline.

For more than a decade, my deepest fear had been my whole family gone, and here it was, entirely possible.

Dad had been working in a high-profile position, but when the state administration changed, his job, in his words, was dismantled. During the preceding years, he had earned a good living. My mother had started working at a magazine, as she had before I was born. My father had a new group of friends who doted on Sarah. When I sent my parents a paper I had written that earned an A, Dad was proud. He made photocopies of the essay to show those same friends.

On the phone, Mom explained that she and Sarah would stay in Pennsylvania, close to hospitals in Boston and New York. Sarah should stay in school as much as she could, and Mom would keep working. Someone, she said, ought to be here for me during school vacations. We clung to our habit of dismissing fear by moving too fast for the emotion to sink us. Sitting on my floor, clutching the receiver, I could not help but notice that I was afraid.

"Are you scared?" I asked.

"Not now, but I was an hour ago, and I will be tomorrow," she answered. Mom had the same sneaking sensation of freedom that I did. Without my father present, we could speak our minds.

"We are still a family," my mother said. "A family of four very separate and separated people."

She had been given her break, and Dad had been given his. As in every family crisis since Susie's death and my father began to fall apart, Mom was resolutely unsentimental. If she fell apart, too, she reasoned, who could Sarah and I turn to?

My mother grew up believing that good parents stayed together, raised children, shared decisions and responsibilities. She had been her parents' pet, encouraged and sheltered. Her mother ran the household, but her father was in charge. As a bride and young wife, my mother assumed that life with my father would be calm and unified, as her parents' marriage had been. She would be the wife who raised care-free children; my father would be the even-keeled husband steering a course toward his family's happy camaraderie.

I wonder now when my mother recognized that Dad had stopped steering. She saw it in Jamaica, marooned in a make-believe vacation. She saw it at home, when Dad, inca-pacitated by depression and drugs, stayed in bed for days and nights, interrupted by manic bursts of writing on a wall or threatening to jump from the roof. The day my father de-cided to move to Singapore, my mother's only choice was to take the wheel.

That night, I tried crystal meth for the first time, be-cause I needed something to do.

When the lease on their house expired, Mom found an apartment the right size for a mother and daughter. She sold some furniture to lighten her move, shedding weight from her old life. I think now that half a world's distance helped my parents loosen their hold on one another. They each put a toe in separate waters, and learned that they were stronger apart.

Early in his sojourn, perhaps on his way overseas—the letter is written on Pan Am airlines stationery—my father explains to my mother his conviction that living in Asia is the right thing for him, a chance to learn "what matters," and to remove himself from what he calls "obsessive worry-ing" about Sarah.

My father sent money; his letters often began with "Enclosed is the monthly check," although at times, he asked my mother to pay credit card bills, adding that he is becoming "disciplined" about spending money. His love of the exotic in his letters from this period is clear. The same urge that pulled him to Jamaica ten years earlier was powerful in Singapore. He wrote about luxury hotels and "big deal receptions," sent postcards of temples and jungles, and wrote about the humor he found in being served a version of lox and bagels, typical Jewish Sunday brunch fare even in the Far East.

Living her nonexotic life, my mother was happy: free to make her own friends, speak her mind, and care for Sarah in the way she thought was best.

In college, I majored in communications. My declared interest in cameras and microphones mystified my parents. They had been English majors, and viewed my choice as suspiciously as if I had gotten a vocational tech degree.

Instead, I learned how to make movies and television shows. I had never been a movie buff, but my high school required an internship during senior year, and I spent mine in the news department of a local television station. My supervisor was a rotund man addressed in southern style only by the initials of his first two names, given to cracking alarming and racist jokes about the reporters' Chinese takeout dinners. Egg rolls were deep-fried grill scrapings. Chow mein and moo shu were food that offered a new "slant" on dining. No one argued; they took their square cardboard containers and splintery chopsticks from the deliveryman and hunkered down at their desks and editing consoles. During the afternoons that I was there, my supervisor parked me beside the police scanner and told me to holler if anything happened. Not much did, or if there were four-alarm fires and homicides on my watch, I overlooked them, not understanding the numeric codes that squawked through the speaker. When I wasn't listening to firefighters and cops, I rode shotgun with the consumer reporter in the station's sedan. While the reporter queried money-laundering loan companies, I settled into the passenger seat, sucked melting ice from my soda cup, and fantasized about being a reporter and doing "stand-ups" of my own, counting down until the camera rolled, then signing off by saying my name and the TV station's slogan.

In television production classes, an effort as minor as learning how to coil heavy electrical cables on a practice set or hauling a video camera and a microphone into a subway station for a class project was a laboratory experiment in pushing people around. The hierarchy was simple. The director was the sun and the rest of the crew the solar system. As planets with assigned tasks, we moved closer and farther from the sun, sometimes imploding, other times flaring like a new star. I wanted to be the sun. Television radiated power more magnetic to me than love.

I moved to Los Angeles as soon as I could after my senior year was over. I wanted a new, blank page in my life, the same ceremonial feeling I got when I bought a new journal and a pen with the right kind of easy-flowing ink. I craved a gesture that would tear my past and future in two.

My father's job in Singapore ended after a year. When he came back to the States, my parents started divorce proceedings, without a fight, and my father moved to Los Angeles. Sarah and I had expected them to break up for years. When they finally did, we felt as though we had averted a storm.

The airline ticket to Los Angeles was the first one-way ticket I had ever held. I kept it in my canvas backpack on my bedroom doorknob, and checked it several times a day, sliding my fingers into the cardboard envelope and over the thin paper inside. The idea of leaving for good thrilled me in a way that was portentous and promising. No one else I knew was heading to California with their newly minted degrees.

In an attempt to re-create myself as a free spirit, I divined a new history for myself. In Los Angeles, I would say that I had been halfway to California, watching the Great Plains from an airplane seat thirty-five thousand feet up, before I realized that I had no job prospects and no place to live. (In truth, I was going to stay with my father and his girlfriend for a week or so, and work as an office temp until I got on my feet.) Telling my new history, I convinced myself that I was carefree, brave, and admirably reckless. I was a version of Jessica who never had sisters in the first place, a girl without loss. Los Angeles was the traditional proving ground for false identities. "We are all self-made," I told myself on the pages of my journal.

For the first year I lived in California, I filed paperwork and answered phones at an advertising agency. My manager was kind to me. She did no more than send me home to change clothes when I showed up for work in a grubby

T-shirt with the faded Fiorucci cherub logo across my breasts. Some afternoons, a group of women friends my boss had made from the office retreated to her Spanish-style villa in Beverly Hills to drink champagne cocktails.

Unlike Atlanta, where steamy summertime humidity could make me feel thick and drowsy until the late afternoon cloudbursts cooled the air, the dry heat in Los Angeles made me alert. I had lived through a string of Boston winters, but in California, I felt warmed to the bone and graceful in the way I moved my body. All around me, I found surprises that seemed like lush gifts. An avocado tree dropped ripe fruit on the parking lot behind my apartment building. Lemons and grapefruit trees grew in lawns, their branches scraping windows and carport roofs. The trees were not tended in rows like those in Florida groves. Instead, they were knobby, and sat like shrubbery, the way a small magnolia might look at home. A friend reached out of her window and picked two small grapefruits, one for each of us. We ate the fruit in her kitchen, peeling the yellow skin with our thumbs.

My first solo apartment had one room and a bathroom. I cooked my meals on a two-burner hot plate wedged onto a wooden shelf, and washed my dishes in the bathtub. I slept on a built-in Murphy bed that upended into a closet. I read *Billboard* and *Adweek* and *Variety* and the *Hollywood Reporter*, always starting at the back so that I could circle the employment notices with a red marker. During my first year in California, I carried a growing stack of index cards on which I wrote names, telephone numbers, and notes charting every time I answered an ad or made a cold call, and how many days I would let pass before I called back. My father had given me some names, too: someone from a squeaky-clean family rock band that he said was just waiting to be the next Partridge Family, someone else who was friends with a secretary in the tape duplication department of a network.

When I got my break after a year of index cards and phone calls, I quit the advertising agency for a job on a game show. Every morning I drove from West Los Angeles to Burbank in my sun-bleached red Datsun, whose backseat came loose from its moorings and hit me in the kidneys when I coasted downhill.

My job as a production coordinator was an exercise in optimism. I sat at a metal desk in a row of metal desks occupied by other assistants—the writer's assistant, the talent assistant, an executive secretary—each doing her own tasks, then picking up the phone, putting it down, and sprinting out of our office to her boss's door. I sorted through drawers of contracts with the actors' unions that had never been organized properly. I pulled the top sheets from the middle sheets, and sent the bottom sheets away in interoffice envelopes. I was entrusted with solving problems that had been left to fester. They were easy fixes compared to the irreparable damage that existed in my family. Here, I could make things right.

By the time I had lived in Los Angeles a year, I kept brown glass vials of cocaine at work. Top left desk drawer, next to the marker pens and the staple remover. My left pinkie nail was long and trough shaped, the perfect scoop. If you didn't have coke in your drawer, you had a bottle of vodka in your credenza. Production days at a studio can be extraordinarily long. At one production company, the vitamin B-12 lady came to the conference room every Wednesday at noon. If you weren't scared of needles, you could take your turn, drop your drawers, and get a boost to get you through the week.

A television show in production is choreographed as meticulously as a ballet. Cameras on wheels and mechanical cranes skim past one another on the studio floor with the concentrated grace of ice skaters. The director and the assistant directors sit in a soundproof control room that's often a level above the studio, watching every camera's movement on video monitors, coaching the camera operators through their next move, listening to every word the actors say, checking the spoken word against the written scripts. Every angle of every shot has been planned and practiced, and like a good parent, the director's role is the omniscient eye, making sure that nothing fails in his care. Camera 2, ready for a close-up; camera 1, pull back for a wide shot. Glide and cruise. In the control room—the "booth"—crew members surround the director, calibrating knobs and levers, fading the music cues up and down, cueing the tapes that play the prerecorded commercial announcements. There is never a fraction of a second to spare.

Even the craft services table, where Tootsie Rolls, coffee, and sparkling water are dispensed to anyone with permission to be on the set, can be the fulcrum of the universe. Without the skim milk or 2 percent milk or half-and-half for the coffee and the black jelly beans from the cut-glass bowl, an entire show can lose its secret rhythm. As the production coordinator, I had the keys to the petty cash box and a production assistant or two to send out to bring back the candy or the right kind of cream for coffee that the craft services kid (and it was usually a kid, someone a little younger and newer to the studio than you) will use to pacify the producer. In the greenroom, the hospitality room where the actors—always called talent—snack and chat and wait for their cues, you have to know the personalities involved, who likes to joke around and who won't speak to you. This one's wearing thigh-high leather boots; that one's an animal rights activist. Keep them apart.

The bigger the star, the nicer they are, the saying goes. I carried spare copies of contracts and the release forms for civilians—the nonpros who show up in a bumper shot, that shot of the studio audience applauding right before the commercial break because the electric sign at the front of the room flashes "applause." I didn't always collect every signature, because I could only be in so many places at once. As keeper of the shooting schedule on a variety show, I wore a big headset or a walkie-talkie to hear from the director that the segment with the teenage actress discussing her rehab has been canceled. Time for a schedule change. Tell the comedian he can go longer by three minutes. Tell the teleprompter guy we're getting him new copy. Tell everyone you're getting new scripts for the whole cast. Run back to the office; fly back to the office. Finally, a world that could not turn without me.

I lived and worked in Los Angeles for four years on three shows at studios in Hollywood and Burbank. In one hundred–degree weather, I wore a down vest at work, because soundstages are cavernous and cold. Sitting in a metal folding chair in the half-darkness, I sorted the sheet music for the next show and numbered the comedian's cue cards. Behind gated walls and past toll booth–sized guardhouses, Hollywood-studio back lots span entire city blocks. They are concrete islands of office buildings, commissaries, and soundstages, traversed by golf carts.

On the lot, I scurried from studio to office, where over time I ran hundreds of thousands of script pages through the copier: white for the first draft, green for the next round of changes, pink, yellow, blue for more and more revisions. Looking for a late-arriving star, I ran to stage 14, stage 21, once past a propman pushing a grocery cart heavy with live iguanas. This appealed to me so much that I stopped to watch. Here was a moment nothing like real life: pebble-fleshed, spiny lizards ferried across a scorching Hollywood back lot by a man as somber as a night-shift orderly with a wheelchair. I neither knew nor asked if the iguanas were a variety show act or were on their way to their close-ups in a monster movie. They were just there, part of my new real life where strange was normal, and one thing was as irregular as the next.

One night, as Gregg Allman taped a segment with the show's house band, my longing for the easygoing attitudes and the swaying spoken rhythms in the South, where my sisters and I were girls, rose up from the place I had shoved it in my heart, and I lay my head on my desk and cried.

. I had deliberately segregated myself from my past by moving to Los Angeles, putting as much distance as I could between myself and the people and places that defined me. The kinds of separation I was familiar with were total: either you moved away or you died.

In trying to become someone new, I stepped further along the precipice I first ventured onto in college. When I left Boston, I could have moved to New York—less than a day by train from my mother's house in Harrisburg—but that was familiar ground. Learning who I was meant doing a version of what my father had done, although I did not realize then how similar our actions were. I didn't leave the country, but I went to the farthest ocean.

In California, my father lived less than an hour from me, but he was an awkward version of the father he had been when I was young, and I usually avoided him. I lived twenty-four hundred miles from Sarah and Mom, and I saw them only when I flew back to Pennsylvania on Thanksgiving or New Year's. I missed my little sister and my mother more than I would admit. At twenty-two, I was negotiating the divide between childhood and adulthood, unsure if I was my mother's equal or a little girl who needed guidance.

I expended megawatts of energy not thinking about the sounds of my mother's and sister's voices, or the joyous way my heart lifted when we were together. When I was with them, I relaxed and got funny, stepping comfortably into family mode alongside my mother's mordant wit and my sister's labyrinthine imagination. We made lists of imaginary words, starting with "pighetti," pasta for an orange-felt finger puppet of a pig Sarah treasured from childhood. We dissected and evaluated the secret lives of Mom's coworkers, of the Mennonite women selling baked goods at the farmers' market, and Sarah's teachers.

If I admitted to myself, or my family, that I missed them even a little bit, my reinvention mission would fail. So I ignored my longing to run home. The same way Mom willed herself not to weaken when Susie died or when my father moved away, I refused to look backward. If I gave in, I would collapse. I was operating on instinct, struggling to create the new version of me, the girl with no past. I never completely forgot that I had lost one sister and would likely lose another before too many years would pass, but I couldn't allow myself to dwell there. I could not bear to think about my mother when I dipped into this scenario, and so I blanked her out.

Living in Los Angeles made me feel as if I were bursting out of my skin. Burritos and tacos and falafel were saltier, water sweeter, beer colder. In daylight, I saw in sunlight yellow and bougainvillea pink and eucalyptus green. Cocaine seared my sinuses and made my heart pound double time in the seconds before I tipped my head back to let the residue drip, caustic and gritty, the way freshly poured concrete must taste, down the back of my throat.

With friends from work and parties, I played volleyball on Sunday mornings in a dewy green park outside the Twentieth Century Fox studio lot. We carried sandwiches in coolers. The men wiped their sweat with their T-shirts, and eventually took them off, tossing the shirts as wads of color on the ground. Men had a physical casualness I found foreign. I eyed their bare stomachs and chests, and worked on my serve. When my turn came to play the front line, I was dangerous, jumping away from the anger and confusion in my body as I charged toward the hurtling ball.

For the first time since high school, I let myself become interested in men. In college, I fancied myself too mean to care about romance. If a boy was flirtatious or suggestive with me, I led with a hostile attitude and implied that I would follow with my fists. In college, I dressed to hide—adding men's hiking boots and oversized work shirts to what Mom called my bag-lady look. Happy with my pack of friends, I was content to play my guitar, smoke joints, and read. I didn't date in college, and told myself I didn't want to. In Los Angeles, the new me emerged, starved for attention, and I fell for men savagely.

I fixed my attention on a studio musician I barely knew. I stayed home one night to watch a melodrama on television only because he was in it. The scale of my infatuation fascinated me, and I made of myself a reassuringly clinical experiment. The closeness with which I watched every move made by the character on the screen was the symptom of a disease. The disease flared up when I scrutinized the man's face. I compared his expression, comforting an actress, against how he had looked chatting with me during a studio meal break. This is what couples were supposed to look like, the caring man devoted to the woman in need. No slamming doors, no angry silences.

One night, after standing across a room and watching my musician leave a party without speaking to me, I wryly celebrated my social failure by treating myself to a gram of coke. For the rest of the night, I chopped out lines at the host's kitchen table, and shared my reward with no one.

I fell into bed with one man or another in the early morning hours when parties waned. Afterward, I made my excuses, gathering my things and escaping for home. If we were at my apartment, I pretended to listen as the man pretended to promise to call. As his car started up outside in the dark, I'd thank no one in particular that he'd left. Sometimes I simply made a date with a gay friend to curl up together on his bed for an intimate evening of television and popcorn.

I moved with a pack, to parties thick with self-conscious whimsy, where couples dressed as Rob and Laura Petrie from *The Dick Van Dyke Show*, and others where we were invited to dress as warm-weather Santa Clauses. I went to backyard luaus where friends who were in about-to-be-famous bands played rockabilly and Paisley Underground rock and some of us shot Super 8 film and others wore brassieres made of coconut halves. After work, with minutes to go until midnight, I went to Madame Wong's to see Los Lobos, or to the Cathay de Grande, a block south of

Hollywood Boulevard, to see the Long Ryders. I dyed my hair eggplant-purple. It seems now that I never, ever slept.

I rarely saw my father. As far as I knew, he never ventured into Hollywood or to the rolling miles of gated studios in Burbank and Studio City. Sometimes when I was on the west side, I stopped by his office, but he irritated me. He talked about his girlfriend's daughter's upcoming part in a hit sitcom, and how much I would like her. He got all of us together one afternoon, my father and me, the girlfriend and her daughter. The daughter talked, but in my mind, I only heard the theme song from her television show. After lunch, I was asked to drive her to see her agent. While I drove through traffic in Beverly Hills, she jerked my rearview mirror toward the passenger seat and freshened her lipstick. My father was trying to create another version of family, without the right players.

I spent a few afternoons with my father on the boardwalk in Venice Beach. He ambled and I strode. He prolonged time; I accelerated it. Instead of talking about Sarah, or our dissolved family life, we must have talked about books, or politics, or the California life we saw in front of us. We watched a street performer juggle chain saws, and tourists turn browner and slicker in the salt air. I checked my watch and counted the minutes until I could get away and turn back to my own life.

Averting my eyes from my family, I tried to create a self that I could see. On a page of my journal in soft pencil, tentative as a whisper, I wondered to myself, "Is this how normal people live their lives?"

Mom wrote to me regularly, chatty, easygoing letters in which she addressed me like an equal. I was her daughter, but I was also a grown woman and a trusted friend: her fellow traveler, in a way. In some letters, she chose not to mention Sarah at all. You exist, and I do, too, was written between the lines.

My mother visited once, on a trip to California for work. I drove her around and showed off my world: women groomed like show cats shopping Rodeo Drive, the dusty-green hills leading to the Hollywood sign, the odd truth that facing west meant the end of land and the beginning of sea, rather than the other way around. We grocery shopped, filling my refrigerator with cheeses, bread, and strawberries that Mom said were as big as an infant's fist. We shopped in home decor stores near Melrose Avenue, and fell in love with heavy folk-art Italian dinner plates with Romano, Positano, Gallo d'Oro painted around the rims. Whether they were cities or restaurants, we didn't know, but the staccato words appealed to our escapist desires.

When we hugged good-bye at the airport, I had a sudden urge to leave with her. Instead, I did what a lifetime had ingrained in me: I blamed the urge to cry on my sinuses. Mom waved and walked to her gate, and I drove to the studio. We parted ways not like a mother and daughter who missed one another, but as two adults who had conceded to the rules of compromise.

When Sarah visited, the two of us were inseparable, giggling uncontrollably, buoyant with sisterly intimacy. I didn't think of Susie or let myself imagine what this L.A. visit would be like with three sisters together. I succeeded, most of the time, in putting Susie out of my mind. Sarah was seventeen, and because it was the normal thing to do, because perhaps her luck would change and she could live a healthy life, she had applied to college.

Even though her life was no longer a daily part of mine, and I had put almost three thousand miles between us, I lived hard enough for her and me and for Susie, too. Three lives in one. I had enough strength for three with my portion of power on the set—my schedules, my headsets, and my Rolodex with celebrity home phone numbers. I had enough strength for three with my portion of power outside the studio gates—a pocket mirror, a razor blade, and a hearty hug from a bona fide rock-and-roll star inside the private after-hours club. My power in these places was within my control. There was nothing I could do for Sarah except be her sister.

part three

Jessica, Atlanta, 1968

11.

I have dreamed of my childhood home almost since the day I left it. I dream of begging the new owners of our family's home to let me in. I dream of the kitchen or the laundry room or the den, never my bedroom or Sarah's or the walk-in cedar closet with off-season clothes hanging beneath a bare yellow bulb with a pull chain. I dream of the rooms that were shared, not the ones into which we retreated, licking our wounds.

My mother dreams of butchers. Now that I am grown and have asked her what the years of Susie's and Sarah's illnesses were like for her, she tells me about the images her subconscious has made. In these dreams, she sits on the front steps of a house, waiting for someone to come from inside and let her in. When the door opens, my mother finds herself peering into the kitchen of our Atlanta home, through a window in a door that was never there. On the *other side of the door are white tile walls misted with blood. Thick steel hooks hang empty from the ceiling, and a metal work table straddles a floor drain. In the abattoir, a butcher stands alone, wiping his heavy knife clean on his apron.*

The house we grew up in became the symbol of what should have been. When we moved in, Susie was well. My father was well. Sarah was sick, but as a family, we were innocent of how her illness would harm each of us. When I returned to Atlanta to live as an adult, I found that I drove aimlessly past that house regardless of my intended destination. Sometimes this detour took me miles out of my way, but I could not dispense with it.

When I left Los Angeles, I returned to Boston for a few years before making my way back to Atlanta. One day I was simply tired of Los Angeles, where everyone sized each other up according to how they looked, who they knew, and what they did for a living. I wanted to live where seasons changed, and my mother and sister were closer than an overnight flight.

Although I was not yet ready to move all the way back to my childhood home, I had never entirely let it go. With each move, I stayed in touch with some of my oldest friends. In college, I was thrilled to get a gift in the mail from a high school pal: a shoe box packed full of green pods of fresh southern okra, with homegrown pot snuggled in foil beneath the top layer of vegetables. After college, I traveled south periodically, where I'd stay with my old friend Mary Beth and hang out with friends from school. Each time, I left convinced that I had to make my adult home any place other than where my sisters and I had been children.

Every time during the years I returned to visit my friends, I wept. I sobbed on airplanes. I cried on Amtrak. I didn't know what I was crying about: I told myself I was tired.

Images of myself and Susie and Sarah as little girls ran like a slide show behind my eyelids. Susie and me wriggling on the hard chairs in our doctor's office waiting room, sucking lollipops on looped strings, pretending we were eating worms. Sarah and me at the kitchen table, having after-school snacks and doing homework, Sarah opening her mouth to expose chunks of chewed food guaranteed to make me squeamish.

I refused to make the connection between my memories and my grief. For years, I kept a typewritten list that I had made during a concentrated afternoon of self-examination. I made the list long after college, between jobs, trying to locate my center. The list was called "Atlanta: Pro and Con." My reasons for moving back—or not—ran neck and neck down three eight-and-a-half-by-eleven pages. "More oriented to settling down" was under the pro side. "Could be hard," argued the con side. "Old & New people" on the pro side. "So what?" taunted the con. In 1989, the pro side won, and I moved back.

Sarah came to visit me the year I moved back to the place we reflexively called home. She asked me only once to drive past our old house. I parked across the street under the shade of the neighbor's Bradford pear tree, and we sat in my car as if hypnotized, watching the sun dapple the pine trees on the wide lawn. It felt like we were revisiting the scene of a crime. I held my breath. Sarah reached forward and turned the car radio off.

The shutters on the house looked recently painted—beige, instead of the black they had been. New shingles made the gable over the attic window look bright and cheerful. A screened porch extended around the back of the house from what had been Sarah's bedroom. The camellia bushes in the front yard and the azaleas along the driveway had been shorn.

Watching a red brick ranch house, we were searching for ourselves, and for answers. How would we be different if we had grown up free of the shadow of loss that stalked us? What would we have been like as a family?

Asking if a person has brothers and sisters is an ordinary question. Most people never think twice about how to answer. For years, I examined my answers. Should I spare the inquirer's feelings and soft-pedal my response? How would I do that and still be truthful? Lying would be efficient, but disloyalty to Susie and Sarah was unbearable.

The life and motion of my family had ceased to be about me in 1968, the year Susie got sick. My perception of my father's work began to turn from watching him make a better world for his children to championing people I perceived as stand-ins for my sisters, individuals with problems that could be solved. These drug addicts, runaways, and, later, refugees were to me a faceless pack I viewed as "them," the broken who were not my family.

I no longer knew what it was like to be me without one and, later, both sisters. As the well sibling, I withdrew from and then I ran from my family. Discovering for myself the story of my sisters—and myself—is how I chose to come home.

By the time Sarah and I staked out our childhood home, I had graduated from college and was well into my working life. Sarah had a job and a boyfriend. She and Mom had moved to Boston, and Sarah lived in a glossy apartment in a restored Victorian house in Dorchester, blocks from the duplex our mother rented. A few years before, Sarah had started college in Rhode Island, but had to come back to our mother's house before the end of the first semester. Dorms breed infections, exhaustion, and illness.

Before she started college, she had been accepted to a prestigious summer creative-writing program. A week before class started, she had to withdraw; painful abscesses emerged in her jaw. Her chin swelled to the size of the rest of her face. These losses reminded us that the span and scope of my sister's life were measured differently. My parents expected victories from me. I waved the thought away like a bad smell.

During Sarah's trip to Atlanta, we visited Egleston Hospital for Children, at Sarah's request.

"How about Egleston?" she asked, browsing through my bookshelves.

The route to the hospital was as familiar to us as the one to school. At the hospital, the automatic doors slid aside with a graceful hush. Inside, we walked the halls to the left and right of the lobby, browsed in the gift shop, smelled the boiled smell of the cafeteria. In the lobby, we looked at the oil paintings of benefactors and then walked out the back door into the garden, with the same pathways and statuary where twenty years earlier Susie had blown out the candles of her eighth birthday cake. We passed a wall of plaques listing the names of children whose parents had made gifts to the hospital.

"All those names," Sarah mused.

Craning her head back, she read every one of them, looking for people she had known, kids with whom she had played backgammon or Crazy Eights in the playroom. "My name's not there," she mused.

"Yeah," I said. "But you lived."

I saw clearly from her disgusted expression that I had disappointed her. I was ignorant, still, of the weight of Sarah's guilt.

Sarah knew from childhood that her illness put our family under strain. She saw this in our parents' stress. She saw this in the bills that came in the mail. Every school day she missed—and she missed weeks at a time—and every slumber party or school dance she couldn't attend made her feel different, and perhaps diminished. I went away to college, yet she was unable to finish. She was often nauseated from medication, and sore from infections and incisions. Sarah may have felt that our father's leaving, and even mine, was because of her. Her worry was one more thing we didn't discuss as a family. Like me, she kept her fears to herself.

When Sarah was in high school, a new principal who had screened her absence records called her into a truants' assembly. Mistakenly lumped into a group of kids with bad attitudes, Sarah was upbraided for her poor attendance. She came home from school late that day, infuriated. Mom called the principal, and explained Sarah's situation. The principal apologized, and as with so many adults in her life, became my sister's advocate.

Every time Sarah was in the hospital, she made friends with pharmacists, nurses, doctors, lab technicians, playroom workers, and patients. These kids sometimes went home, as Sarah did, "sprung from the slammer," in our family jail-house slang, and sometimes they died. Sarah mourned them quietly.

As Sarah and Susie's sister, I looked outward, away from myself. My watchfulness, what psychologists would later call hypervigilance, spread after my father climbed the roof. What, I wondered, do people make of us? What do they make of me? Me, growing tall and curvy, five foot seven and a half with a thirty-seven-inch bust and a twenty-seven-inch waist at the age of thirteen (how carefully I measured myself, counting even the smallest hash marks on the yardstick and the tape measure, and dreading every new fraction of an inch). Me, recording my measurements with clinical detachment in my rounded handwriting on a lined journal page. I was too tall, too chesty, too olive skinned. Too for whom I didn't know. Too for me, comparing myself with my stunted and fragile sister, pigeon-chested from limited lung function, blonde haired and a little more than half my height, so fair skinned that blue veins sometimes showed in her wrists.

I was a compulsive journal keeper in my teens, filling one hundred–sheet spiral notebooks at the rate of one every month or two. My journal entry from March 28, 1974, has a rare quality: I observed my family and directly addressed the effect of Sarah's health on our lives. On that page, I wrote that Sarah was "admitted to the hosp on Sat and went into brain surgery on Tuesday." As was usual for Sarah, one infection had led to another, but this time her brain was inflamed: surgeons removed a piece of her skull behind her right ear to drain the infection. Reading now that I was "v. upset of course but partly I think for show," I see myself at fourteen, crying at the news that Sarah would have to have such serious surgery. I remember, too, pushing my tears and crying theatrically, making dramatic gasps through my sobs to prove to my parents, and to me, that I cared.

I did not ask myself what I made of me. I had learned to look at my family through peekaboo fingers, afraid of what I would see. My fear was rewarded every time, and so I stopped looking. I began, instead, to build new families for myself wherever I could find them.

12.

The specimen submitted to Pathology showed a male
fetus approximately 16 to 18 weeks gestation. [Sarah]
was seen in follow-up by the Gynecology service
. . . . Psychiatry service provided supportive care.

—Discharge summary,
Memorial Sloan-Kettering Cancer Center

As Sarah and I grew up, I became responsible for opening
the door to her bad behavior. When I was fourteen and
Sarah nine, Sarah and I stood with three of my friends in
the bathroom we shared. The parallel doors to our rooms
were shut tight, and Sarah, who weighed less than sixty
pounds, leaned hard against the door into my room, believing that she was holding it closed and shielding us with her
small frame. The single window was flung open to the sharp
night air. My friends and I passed a skinny joint from hand
to hand, inhaling deeply, dropping our eyelids to half mast,

absorbed in the mystique of holding the smoke in our lungs. When we were ready to choke, we stepped up onto the toilet seat and rested our chins on the windowsill to blow the smoke outside, where its sticky-sweet smell mingled with the piney bite of winter.

Sarah watched us, her eyes big and her mouth slightly open.

Sarah began to list to her left, toward the towel rack. Even though we assiduously blew our smoke out the window, the bathroom had gotten hazy. The four of us watched as Sarah slid in slow motion down the door to the floor, where she landed on her butt with a thud. We busted out laughing. She busted out laughing. My little sister was stoned.

The smoke drifted under the door, down the hall, and to the family room at the other end of the house. My father sniffed the air and rose from the big black chair where he had been reading. In the bathroom, we heard his approaching footsteps and stamped the joint out on the white tile floor before we flushed the roach down the toilet. My friend Liz waved the smoke out the window. Sarah tried to sit up but slid down again, laughing.

Bang! My father's fist hit my door, and Sarah, on the bathroom side, sprawled forward. Bang, and bang again.

"There is a distinct odor of pot in this house!" my father bellowed. He was indignation incarnate, deep voiced and stern.

"Well, he would know," Eleanor whispered. She rolled her eyes. She had taken over the task of clearing the air, waving her arms like a flagman, and ushering wisps of smoke out the window. I was on the floor with a wad of dry toilet paper, wiping the ashes of the stubbed-out joint from the tile grout.

"Just a minute, Dad," I sang out, standing up and pulling Sarah upright by her elbow.

My friends were sent home, dispatched into the cold night. Mom tried to calm Dad.

"Stop acting like a prosecutor, Jack," she said.

My father was a defense attorney, and my mother contended that only when he was home did he behave like a prosecutor—antagonistic and cunning. Turning to me, she told me to quit. Whatever drugs I was doing, just quit them, now. I wondered to myself if I would quit; I didn't care much one way or the other—smoking pot was simply something to do. To my parents I said little, although my father called me a liar and a sneak. He questioned Sarah at the kitchen table, but she kept our secrets. How much were they smoking? Where did they get it? Even under interrogation, Sarah stayed loyal to me.

Confidences are the currency of siblinghood. We trade in secrets, and we lock them away as keepsakes of trust. How many sisters have said, "If I tell you something, you've got to swear never to tell," and how many sisters have placed their hands over their hearts in solemn affirmation?

"If I tell you this, will you swear never to tell Mom?" Sarah said to me one day when she was in high school and I was in Harrisburg, visiting. "Last time I was in the hospital, I coded."

Code blue means that a patient's heart has stopped—on the medical dramas, that's when the attractive intern comes running, pushing a "crash cart" loaded with lifesaving equipment. Sarah was pleased with herself, nonchalantly slinging the language of emergency rooms. I didn't see any reason not to believe her, and I wanted the fifty-cent tour.

"Did you see a white light at the end of a tunnel?" I asked. "Did you hear voices?"

We were fascinated by television shows about the occult. We could always count on one to dramatize the moment of crossing over. On television, the soundtrack of the patient's beating heart rose in volume before it skipped, then slowed to nothing. The image on the screen went from color to supercharged black-and-white, as if we needed a hint about the direness of the situation. And here was Sarah, alive and serious, purporting to have held a round-trip ticket to the other side.

"I heard a nurse shouting, 'She's coding,' and I heard machines beeping," Sarah said. "I was dead, for a minute."

Her narrow escape awed us both.

I can find no mention of an incident like this in her medical records, but I believe my sister. She told me things that mattered.

"I can't have sex with a man if he's got ugly hands," Sarah told me years later.

We were in her apartment, it was late morning, and she was in her pajamas. She was nineteen then, maybe twenty.

"His hands have got to be clean, and he has to take good care of them. I don't want them here otherwise."

She held her breasts together and shuddered, imagining the caress of a man with bitten nails or calluses. A man with hands not like a doctor's.

All I wanted to do after I had sex, I offered, was sleep. Curl up and sleep, or throw the guy out.

"Not me," Sarah said. "I get all this energy, I want to get the hell up and get busy, do something like alphabetize the spice rack."

When did my sister grow up? I wondered.

My boyfriends had incited eye rolling in Sarah. This one was a slob, I had been a suck-up to that one, the one before was not smart enough for me. Sarah's boyfriends were pals first; one had taught her to shoot a rifle. Sarah told me that she and her friends put on orange hunting safety vests and went into the woods to blast beer cans from tree stumps. Boyfriends and girlfriends talked to her for hours on the phone when she was sick in bed. Boys taught her to change the oil in her secondhand Datsun, a car she loved to go "bombing" in, driving so hair-raisingly fast on hills that curved around pastures and the prefab suburbs around Harrisburg that even I, a harum-scarum driver, gripped the dashboard when Sarah was at the wheel.

When Sarah and I were in our twenties, we got pregnant within months of one another. Sarah had just turned twenty-two. Mom told me about Sarah's pregnancy after it was over, her voice flat and detached, as if divesting the story of emotion would make it easier to bear.

Later, when I confided in Sarah that I had chosen not to take my own pregnancy to term, I asked her to promise not to tell Mom. Telling Sarah that I was planning to have an abortion, I thought I was proving to myself that I could be her equal, just once confronting the inner workings of my body and giving myself over to masked strangers with knives.

Susie and I had predicted when we were small that we would both grow up to be mothers. Circumstance had proved her wrong, and I had come to dismiss that vision of my future. Motherhood was the dream of a woman unformed and unhardened. Not me. Not a Mother. Not then, not ever.

For a month, I had chalked my symptoms up to my working conditions. I was twenty-seven, and had moved from Los Angeles back to Boston. I worked for a company that produced television programs, and I was their production manager, keeping track of budgets and schedules. I had flown with the director and a camera crew to an industrial town in New Jersey to tape segments for an upcoming show. My long workdays, I believed, were the reason I was so tired.

When I got back to Boston, my doctor told me that I was pregnant.

My boyfriend lived in a high-rise in Cambridge populated mostly by engineering students. The lobby smelled of burned hair, and flickered under a fluorescent bulb all day and all night. His rent was twice what I earned in a month. I lived with five mismatched housemates in a suburb halfway to Walden Pond. He lived with a dead plant on his concrete balcony and a shower stall full of dirty dishes. When I sat on his couch after yet another dinner out and told him I was pregnant, he proposed that we split the cost of the abortion.

The routine procedure at the clinic was for me to get anesthesia—something local to numb my cervix, Valium to relax me—but I refused. When the nurse pointed her pen at the form that would allow the doctor to sedate me, I realized that I wanted to feel the pain. "No" came from my mouth with such conviction that I seemed to separate from myself, to be both the person who was signing the release forms for an abortion and the person watching her.

"No worse than bad menstrual cramps," my friend Arlene had told me. She had already had an abortion, and she was a nurse; when she described the procedure (over dinner one night I asked her to lead me through it, from beginning to end), I trusted her.

Susie and Sarah each learned ugly and difficult things that I didn't know about living in a body. They were wiser than me by circumstance. I wanted to feel pain in my body.

Lying on the examining table, I took long breaths in and longer ones out. I counted the pinholes in the acoustic tile on the ceiling. My boyfriend had opted to stay in the waiting room.

After I stripped from the waist down and wrapped my lower half in a white paper gown, I was freezing. Nervous, teeth-chattering cold. Nail beds turning purple under the air conditioner cold. A nurse put fuzzy socks on my feet, and held my hand while a doctor attended to a vacuum cleaner on a rolling table beside me. The machine kicked to life. I felt a tube go inside me and probe deep, felt a string of slight pulls, and then one sharp, deep one. The pain was not terrible in a physical way, but when it was over, I shocked myself by crying.

Afterward, I wanted to look at what I had done, to invoke more punishment in glimpsing the wreckage of a body that came from mine.

"I want to see," I said, pushing myself up on my elbows, letting the paper slide from my knees.

"No, honey, you don't," the nurse countered.

Turning her back to me with a deft body block, she wheeled the vacuum away. I saw blood, and was suddenly certain that I had been pregnant with a boy.

In February of that same year, Sarah went into the hospital to treat an infection on her thigh. Reading the paperwork now guides me through a map of her treatment. The angry tissue on her leg was cut open and drained. Doctors gave her increasingly powerful antibiotics and a blood transfusion. The hospital's pain service consulted on treating what they called her "extreme" pain, I assume from inflamed nerves and tissue. When I turn to the second sheet, my real sister flickers to life from the page. Examining her because of "persistent" abdominal cramps, the doctor calls the exam "difficult"—the patient is tense. I see Sarah as she was in her early twenties. She pressed her mouth closed in annoyance, a mirror of our father's tense gesture. Sarah must have known she was pregnant.

At first, no doctor would believe what was happening. My mother has told me only the barest story. Sarah had stronger menstrual cramps than she had ever had before.

The cramping went on into the night, until Mom recognized in horror that Sarah, who was moaning and clutching her middle, was miscarrying. Mom went for a doctor. I imagine her at the nurses' station, slapping her hand flat on the countertop and demanding help.

In her room, Sarah, doubled over, with an IV taped to her hand that dripped antibiotics to treat her infected thigh, got out of bed and went to the toilet. Sitting in the bright light, weeping in pain, the red call button at her knee and the IV pole in the doorway, she miscarried.

In the week that followed, Sarah's abdominal pain returned—her uterus had become infected. Doctors argued about what they should do. Probably no patient with Kostmann's had lived long enough to become pregnant before. Probably because Sarah's periods were irregular and her physical development idiosyncratic, no one had considered that sexual activity would produce the normal outcome.

She had a boyfriend she adored: the baby had been his. Of the two of us, Sarah was the sister who held her arms out to welcome friends' and strangers' newborns, while I recoiled, closing my throat against their milky scent and fearing for their fragile necks. Being a mother was a role that Sarah's unreliable body spirited away.

Had we broken with family convention and faced our lost and discarded pregnancies, I might have known how Sarah felt. Had we been able to start over at our square one, we would have been aunts, and we would have been mothers.

Secrets are a pact. Some mornings after I had been out all night, I would tell Sarah where I had gone, who I went with, and what we had talked about. If there had been a boy involved, I told her what I thought of him now that he had gone. Later, she did the same with me. A breathless "What was it like?" was our shorthand for "Tell me everything."

The night that Sarah died, I wanted to grab her by the wrist and tug her into a seat across from me for a hushed sister-to-sister talk.

"So," I wanted to ask. "So tell me about dying. What was it like?"

13.

Day 8: I have been handed a gift and I am over-whelmed. It seems limitless, a ticket to freedom, keys to the world. An unbelievable thing called a miracle has occurred in a long and difficult struggle. I am so afraid to accept it on even the most superficial level. Part of me is all too aware that this is a reward long overdue . . . but the more realistic, cautious side of me is not willing to breathe a sigh of relief yet, if ever.

—Sarah's journal, 1987

A prescription medication is available now for white cell–impaired patients, those who, for example, have the kind of neutropenia that you can get from certain types of chemotherapy. This drug didn't exist when Sarah first became ill. This drug was created, in part, from Sarah's tests with what one of her physicians dubbed "the G."

By 1987, Sarah agreed to participate in the clinical trials of a newly developed medication. The drug was expected to stimulate white-cell growth in patients who were lacking the ability to produce mature white cells. Sarah had been an informed participant in her medical care since elementary school, and when she turned twenty-one, hers was the final word. She agreed to experiment with the study of a treatment before it went on the market, and she got no argument from our parents. Like her, they were willing to try anything.

Sarah consented to be what she called a "hostage guinea pig," "hostage" describing her stay in a hospital when she was feeling well. She agreed to have a tube surgically implanted near her collarbone—a direct line so that blood could be drawn several times a day without a technician searching her veins each time for a fresh spot for the needle—to have her skin scraped regularly and the cells counted under a microscope. Ultimately, she agreed to help test a remedy that so far had been tried on rats, dogs, mice, and a monkey in a lab.

At the time Sarah began the trial, she and Mom were living in Harrisburg. Dad was in California, and I had returned to Boston. Sarah stayed in the hospital in New York for several weeks before returning home, where she gave herself daily injections. Sometimes she felt well enough to see her friends and go to school. Sometimes, either because of the treatment or because of an infection, she was laid low with body pain, vomiting, headaches, or light-headedness. She took prescription painkillers. Over the course of her life, many of her veins, always small, had gotten difficult to use for injections.

Before she began the testing, Sarah cross-examined her doctors. "The G" was the nickname a physician had given the medication in an effort to domesticate the drug's formal name: *recombinant human granulocyte colony-stimulating factor*. Sarah read the technical summary of the plan of action her doctors would follow. She gave copies of the eighteen-page protocol to each of us, eager to keep us informed. I was grateful to be included, and I was impressed. This was a serious and scholarly undertaking, and Sarah was, in a way, a celebrity. Her illness would no longer be her intimate struggle with her body. The smallest details of how her body reacted to an untried medication would be a matter for science. She was, I think, proud in spite of herself.

One day after surgery in which doctors extracted a sample of her bone marrow and inserted her chest catheter, the first moments of Sarah's science experiment began. The first dose took exactly one hour.

By the tenth day of treatment, she had grown enough neutrophils to be, for the first time, at the threshold of 1,000 cells per microliter: within sight of normal. Five hundred one day, 980 another. Her galloping cell growth began to cause pain: the wide flat bones of her pelvis were unaccustomed to playing host to so much healthy marrow, and her bones felt, as she put it, as if they were stuffed to the rafters. Even with bone pain so severe that walking became difficult, Sarah began to consider the possibility of a new life.

By day thirteen, Sarah's count had dropped again, to 300. When she went home to Pennsylvania she had a system arranged. The local hospital drew her blood once a day and sent the results to her doctors in New York. Every day, too, Sarah stuck a needle in her thigh and gave herself an injection of the G.

By day seventy, her neutrophils were up to 2,000. One day after her twenty-second birthday, my sister was healthier than me.

Day seventy was in early January. But by summertime, Sarah's infections had returned. A swollen jaw, a painful infected eyelid. Her doctors changed her doses. Sarah was on and off the treatment, but in the end, the medication did not work for her. Living with catastrophic illness deprives us of the freedom to be emotional. Otherwise, every day begins and ends exposed to a blow, and every loss and every gain paralyzes. Sarah simply moved on.

I had been feeling excluded from the medical pulse in the center of Mom's and Sarah's lives. As was often true, I wanted something both ways: to be left alone and to be included, to move away, yet stay by my family's side. Not being in my mother's house freed me from direct proximity to Sarah's symptoms, the tension of my mother's worry, and the seesaw effect we felt when Sarah was reasonably well. But it also deprived me of assessing how Sarah was feeling.

When Sarah didn't return my phone calls within a few days, I called Mom. Why assume that Sarah was sick again? I was hearing zebras, not horses, and so I determined arbitrarily that forty-eight hours would prove me calm and rational, not hysterical. Forty-eight hours of shallow breathing and obsessively checking my own answering machine, preparing myself to hear what I knew I would hear someday, that my sister was dead.

If I couldn't reach my mother, then I was certain she and Sarah were both at the hospital in New York. Maybe Sarah went first, taking the train from Harrisburg to Philadelphia and then on to New York, and Mom came later after her office closed for the day, carrying a change of clothes and a briefcase filled with page proofs and articles to edit. Maybe they flew together. I could call patient information at the hospital and ask for Sarah's room, but acting anonymously broke my web of rules.

If my mother did answer her phone at home, I posed tentative questions. "Mom," I said, "do you know where Sarah is? I left a message on Monday, and now it's Wednesday and she hasn't called me back."

Sometimes my mother would be silent, gathering her thoughts, fidgeting with a pencil or a rubber band. Finally, she would answer. "She's been in the hospital a few days." Mom forced herself to sound nonchalant when she said this, as though Sarah were stuck in rush-hour traffic.

"Why don't you tell me when she goes in?" I said. I hollered at my mother, "Why doesn't Sarah call me?"

We didn't want to worry you, my mother said. Someone in this family, she told me again and again, "has to live a normal life."

In the spring of 1988, Sarah had twenty-four teeth removed, radical surgery made more difficult by the fragile, gauzy skin inside her mouth. Sarah's gums had become so infected that her teeth no longer stayed seated. The bones in her jaw were beginning to die off. Each of these problems could trigger an infection poised to spread to her brain, as had happened when she was small. Although she was in her early twenties, the time had come for a full set of dentures.

Sarah began the process of being fitted for dentures after she recovered from surgery. At first, her false teeth didn't fit her well. Her bones were weak and her gums tender, and maybe the prosthesis wasn't well made. Our family jaw is a distinctive one: animate my sisters and me for a Saturday-morning cartoon, and we would be a trio of girl Dudley Do-Rights. Her first dentures made Sarah's face look too long, as if her mouth belonged to someone bigger. A later set of teeth fitted her well. In almost every picture I have that shows Sarah after her second set, there is a nearly imperceptible lift in the corners of her sealed lips.

One afternoon I held my arm out for a nurse, for a rubber strap and a needle, and a tray of glass vials. I had made this physical gesture for the first time more than twenty years earlier, but something, either the strap or the needle or the drawing out of my blood, still made my hand go cold and dead. After my arm was freed and my elbow bent to press a cotton ball and Band-Aid in place, my hand warmed again and prickled to life.

Sarah had asked for my help.

A bone marrow transplant might be the way to go, a new thing to try. Healthy white blood cells taken from someone else and infused into the pulp inside her bones might stimulate Sarah's white cells to grow. Sarah told me this on the phone on a weekend afternoon, she in Boston, me in Atlanta. We talked then at least several times a week. Speaking in a monotone, feigning boredom, Sarah told me about her doctors' transplant idea.

Her nonchalance was a psychological bait and switch. With every new medication and any new test, she and I had come to believe that to divulge excitement was a kind of spiritual incitement for failure. Without planning to, we had developed our own superstition: act like you believe something will work and you can be sure it won't, but pretend you don't care and you might have a chance. When Sarah was well, nearly a typical kid but for her daily medications and adult outlook, we could act as if there were no shadow over our family. We kept that shadow away by not remembering Susie out loud, by not voicing regret about our parents' dissolution, by not asking why I had been allowed to move away so early, returning only for quick visits before I removed myself again. We did not speak out loud about a rosy future. We protected ourselves by living in the present, and not looking too far ahead.

Statistically, siblings are likely matches for stem-cell donation. My doctor in Atlanta would send my blood samples by overnight delivery up to Sarah's doctors to test in Boston. Their labs would tell us just how close, cellularly speaking, we were.

"You'll have to spend six months in isolation if we do this," Sarah warned.

We were not gullible. My sister, my mother, and I worked hard at being abnormally cynical, but we did not scorn reasonable options. Sarah's illness had come from some unknown place, and we never knew what might usher it out of our lives. I was practically prostrate with relief at being asked to provide tangible help instead of my usual good-behavior placeholder. Sarah asked me to relinquish my normal life and go into the hospital, and I didn't hesitate. I think now that she said six months to test me, stretching the truth to see if I would break.

I imagined us in adjacent sterile isolation rooms inside an extraordinary hospital, Memorial Sloan-Kettering in New York or the Dana Farber Cancer Center in Boston. In my mind I saw the buildings in cross section, like architectural versions of the clear plastic "Visible Man" toy. There, my blood and marrow would assemble inside my sister. While I paled, she would fill with color. When our sequestered time was up and we walked into daylight on York Avenue on the Upper East Side of Manhattan or Longwood Avenue in Boston, Sarah would be impervious for the first time in her life to the worst things the wind could blow her way.

She interrupted my reverie. "This is going to be harder on you than it is on me."

"I can handle a hospital stay," I told her, defensive.

"That's not what I'm talking about," Sarah said. "When I die, that's what I mean."

I offered her only foolish statements, because I didn't know what else to do. You won't die from this, don't be silly, this will work, this time will save your life.

The antigens in my blood did not match hers. Neither did those of aunts, uncles, cousins, parents, or friends. My mother remembers the likelihood of finding a matching donor outside our family as close to nonexistent.

14.

As a result of her life events, Jessica has numerous issues related to abandonment, grief, and loss.

—Letter from psychotherapist to insurance company
on behalf of Jessica Handler, August 1995

In late 2004 and early 2005, I requested a large portion of my sisters' medical records from several hospitals. The ease with which I could get them surprised me. Sign a form. Have the minor patient's legal guardian or parent cosign the request: even dead, a patient has a right to her privacy. Egleston Hospital's records clerk told me, kindly, that there would be no charge for the research, since one of the two individuals about whom I was inquiring had "expired" there.

Sarah's file at Sloan-Kettering was huge.

"You know," the woman in the medical records office told me, "this is a twenty-five-hundred-page file."

For the briefest of moments, perverse pride overtook me. My family is stranger than yours. We're the strangest ones of all. Then the misery of how to compile a file that size became clear.

"Holy crap," I said, forgetting my intention to stay composed.

The records-department woman, professionally accustomed to bottomless medical histories, seemed a little fazed, too. Before I could apologize for swearing, she joined me. "No shit," she wheezed.

To save space, I requested only summaries and discharge reports, abstracts of a medical life history that Sarah and I had once joked must be bigger than the Manhattan phone book. We had not realized that we were right.

Some of the pages were poor photocopies of old typewritten forms summarizing procedures and prescriptions. Tight knots of doctor penmanship cramped others. Leafing through the stacks, trying to summon the will to read them, I asked myself what I had been looking for when I sought them out, signing the forms and announcing for the first time to strangers and to myself that these people's lives were part of my own.

Medical records offered remnants of days in Susie's and Sarah's lives when their needs took center stage. The moments within those days existed for my sisters and my parents, but were barely anecdotes for me. I wondered how my sisters' lives could have been so similar to mine, and so different.

Reading the medical-speak in Susie's and Sarah's files was like finding myself at home in a country I had long forgotten. Working without a phrase book or a guide, I traveled swiftly, immersed in the language of the studied body. *Afebrile* means "without a fever." Micturition is urination. *Alopecic*: without hair. *Arteriogram, optic fundi, pathogen*— these flinty words lit small sparks in me. They did not tell the whole story, by any means; they bypass the soul to illuminate short excursions into the body. My sisters' bodies defined their lives, and their lives defined mine. In the terse language and metallic syntax I find moments of imagery—the position in which a body is placed for surgery, one girl who is pale, another overweight, a child who is alert, pleasant.

Scouring files filled with details of their days that I had never known, I wept for my sisters for what felt like the first time. There is Sarah, eight years old, afraid of a bone marrow biopsy, carried from the exam room "in father's arms." There is Susie, hallucinating for reasons the attending physician recorded as "somewhat confusing." Maybe her delirium was a side effect of her steroids, her antinausea medication, or her painkillers. Maybe, he noted, her mental state was the result of her "disease process."

This particular report triggered a vision of Susie and me, when she was about seven years old. We had turned our bedroom floor into a mesa to stage the wedding of an Indian princess doll. The wedding guests leaned rigidly against the leg of a chair: two plastic horses beside an Eskimo doll, her hood a corona of fur. Beside her, a doll in a black wool dress spangled with white buttons like stars in a winter sky. As the Indian princess was ready to walk down the aisle, Susie launched an agitated discussion with the air over my right shoulder, blurting random sentences and stray words.

I froze across from her on the floor, my plastic Palomino horse raised in my hand. Her Indian princess doll, dressed in ankle bracelets with bells and buckskin-colored leather sewn with blue plastic beads, drooped to the floor, while Susie yammered on. I had been holding my breath. The skin between my shoulder blades buzzed with fear.

When she stopped, she slid from English into nonsense before she went silent, short-circuited by an invisible blown fuse. I ran screaming for a parent. I had no words for what I saw until thirty-five years had passed.

From Susie's final discharge summary I cannot determine what my father had meant when he told me, the morning after she died, that someone had given Susie "something." He may have meant morphine. He may have meant digitalis that stabilized her heart rate, a feeling that I imagine might be soothing.

"The patient," I read, "required progressively larger and stronger narcotic agents." Her lower back and her bladder caused her pain. During her last hospitalization, those ten days during which I did not see her and walked alone instead to fourth grade every day feeling that my sister had become a phantom limb, she began a new course of radiation, new chemotherapy, and had her bladder irrigated with distilled water to clear her urine of blood clots. My parents were with her, in the kind of pediatric hospital room that I have seen often enough to envision darkened, the pastel-striped curtains pulled shut on the window between the room and the hallway. My mother says she remembers none of it now, which I am glad of.

. ˙ .

But there are times when I wish my mother could remember more details about my sisters' illnesses. She recalls her frustrations with some doctors and alliances with others, battles with insurance companies and pharmacists. She can summon the diagnostic term for the spots on Susie's chest and arms—*petechiae*—and an image of Susie moonfaced from steroids. She can detail the uneasy way she made use of her suspended time while Sarah was in surgery in New York, on an errand from the hospital at York Avenue and Seventy-second Street, to the Doubleday bookstore on Fifty-seventh to pick up two books Sarah had wanted. Another time, she went to the gift shop at the Metropolitan Museum of Art to buy a Georgia O'Keeffe poster Sarah wanted for her hospital room. Tasks like these distracted my mother from becoming mired in her own fears when Sarah disappeared behind operating-room doors.

Which time and why, I asked my mother, did Sarah check herself out of the hospital AMA, or "against medical advice"? Which playroom friend were we imitating when we began our habit, Dad and Mom and Sarah and I, of teasing each other with the nickname "peanut butter head"?

Mom countered by asking me if I remembered the time that Sarah attended a hospital Halloween party, but refused to wear a costume. She was thirteen years old, and she wore her usual attire: a sweatshirt, jeans, and moccasins.

When a favorite doctor, in costume himself, asked her why she wasn't dressed for the holiday, she retorted that she was. "I am a white cell," Sarah said, pulling a serious face. Her costume, like that key element in her body, was hard to detect.

When I ask about my own childhood, my mother is pained by what she perceives as her absence from my life.

"Do you remember the day my period started?" I ask.

I was twelve and well informed about what would happen to my body. I brought her my blue bikini underpants—look, I said, it's happened.

Atavistically inspired, my mother lightly slapped my cheek. "I don't know why I just did that," she marveled, stroking my face.

She hadn't hurt me, but I was amazed. My mother never hit.

"It's a Jewish tradition. It has to do with bringing color back to your face when you lose blood. It's old-fashioned."

Her mother had done the same to her.

Judaism, as a culture rather than religion, coursed through my family's blood. Occasional Yiddish words, the sporadic appearance of typically Jewish foods like matzoh or challah bread, and a continuing sense of *tikkun olam*—repair of the world—helped guide us. The few Jewish rituals we knew were as natural and as inexplicable to us as illness.

Blood tests displayed hard times coming and going. Genes shaped faces, colored hair, and traced the lines of constancy, as did a mothering gesture from another century. Memories lived in our blood.

15.

Go get 'em!

—Note from my mother to me, early 1980s

I am the oldest child and first daughter, same as my mother. We are both bossy. We presume ourselves always on the right side of an argument. First children appoint themselves leaders, the ones who know what's best for everyone else. A first child, at least until the next one comes along, is also an only child. Even now I believe that I am not an only child: my sisters and I lived part of our lives together, so my "only-ness" is by default.

My mother and her younger brother grew up blocks away from the Atlantic Ocean, in a suburb on Boston's South Shore. In the summer, the air held the low-tide smell of sulfur and mud and seaweed. When the tides were in, my mother, her brother, and neighborhood kids waded into the green water, first to their ankles, then to their knees, the bravest ones going in as deep as their hips. When the tides went out, they dug for clams. Seagulls dropped the clams like stones on the roofs of houses, breaking the shells apart, and swooping down to eat the meat. Their cries sounded shrill and sassy.

By the time she was five years old, my mother began going into Boston with her father on Saturday mornings. They rode in from Quincy, stepping off the last of the two streetcars and two buses at Park Street, near the Boston Common and the gold-domed statehouse. Her father walked with her from there to her piano lesson at a townhouse in the Back Bay. She learned to play Bach's *Anna Magdalena* notebook and later made her way through the sand-colored Schirmer's practice books. Her father waited in the foyer, smoking his pipe and reading the *Boston Globe*.

Afterward, they had lunch in a deli downtown. He ordered an egg salad sandwich for her and a bigger meal for himself. He wished that she would eat more and plump up. All her life, my mother has resembled a Modigliani painting: dark hair and shadowy planes of cheekbones, her knees and elbows sharp angles on long bones.

They spent the afternoon at the Museum of Fine Arts. When the weather was good, they trawled antique stores on Charles Street and in the West End.

Before they left Boston and returned to the shell-lined streets of houses by the sea, her father walked with her to the shops tucked into the brownstones around the pocket parks of Beacon Hill. He bought lavish art books, always used, always cheap. A twelve-volume set of *Scheherazade*, translated by Sir Richard Burton, "absolutely the one to have," my mother remembers. He bought lap-sized anthologies of fairy tales, illustrated with the graceful and slightly bug-eyed characters of Arthur Szyk.

In his soul, her father was a jeweler and an artist. He had emigrated with his parents and siblings from Russia to Woburn, Massachusetts, at the beginning of the last century, arriving in America when he was ten. His first job was helping his father in his failed attempt to farm tomatoes. In his teens, before the Great Depression, my grandfather was admitted to the Massachusetts College of Art—a talented sculptor even then—but he never enrolled. Instead, he worked full-time to help support his parents and five siblings still at home. He worked his entire adult life as a draftsman at the Fore River Shipyard in Quincy, Massachusetts.

When he was retired, in his basement workroom at home, he could turn a chunk of lapis lazuli into a blue scarab the size of a walnut. He carved wood and gesso and wax into replica masks of ancient Japanese men, their earlobes pendulous as upside-down thumbs. He had learned these images and the history that made them real from library books and his Saturday afternoons in museums.

After years of subscribing to *Sky and Telescope Magazine*, my grandfather wrote away to the Carl Zeiss company to buy a heavy glass lens. While he waited for the lens, the telescope's housing perched in the yard. Neighborhood children rolled apples down the center, and called it a cannon. When the lens arrived, my grandfather inserted it into the telescope and pointed it at the moon.

When Susie got sick, my grandparents moved to Atlanta to be near us. Just like we had been when we first arrived in the South, they were fish out of water. My Russian grandfather mowed his lawn shirtless, his suit pants belted high above his waist. He wrapped his head in an ice-soaked towel to fend off the swampy heat.

In his spare time, my grandfather made us a menorah, using quarter-inch copper plumbing line. We put the menorah on the dining room table at Chanukah, and protected the table from multicolored candle drippings with a square of aluminum foil. Like almost every other house on our street, we had seven nights of small gifts (doll clothes, school supplies, or hair bands) and an eighth night with a big gift (a skirt, a book, calendars with stickers). We said no prayers. Instead, Dad intoned the same phrase he used at Passover. "They tried to kill us, we won, let's eat," he said. Thus released, my sisters and I tore into our presents.

Later, our grandfather built music boxes for his three granddaughters. He bought purple amaranth wood from an art supply catalog. He made decorative handles for each box; for Sarah's, he carved a fish from butter-colored ivory, and for mine, a butterfly from pale, seawatery jade. Susie's music box was a silver-mounted orb as big as an ostrich egg, styled like a Fabergé egg.

Susie died before he installed the mechanics.

Each handle, before it was mounted on the box, fitted neatly in an adult palm. Sarah and I opened and shut our music boxes to hear quick fillips of music, amazed and a little alarmed by the elegant casings. These are too beautiful for us, we thought. They are the only ones like them in the world.

When my grandmother was in her fifties, after she and my grandfather had come to Atlanta and shortly after Susie died, she began to worry about irrational things. If she wiped her counter with bleach last week and set a plate of cookies on it this week, would Sarah or I mistakenly ingest Clorox and die? Crying, Grandma called Mom in the evenings. Sarah had eaten a sandwich at her house earlier, and just now she noticed that the plate was chipped. Had Sarah been choking when she got home? Was her mouth bleeding? She's fine, my mother said. She's doing home-work. She's terminal, my mother was thinking. A chipped plate is the least of it.

My grandmother's fears kept her in her house and drove her to her bed; for a short time, her fears sent her to a mental hospital. Although my grandmother and my father were patients in the same psychiatric institute at almost the same time, we never spoke about it.

The fact of my grandmother's hospitalization sailed neatly on my mental horizon: I couldn't visit her; she needed to rest. This seemed cozy and helpful, and was therefore okay with me. My father's mental state, though, unmoored me. There was no great drama in his hospitaliza-tion; he wasn't taken away by men in white coats, hadn't made Halloween shrieks, or grown his nails into spears. I don't know, actually, how the news came to me that he was going to spend a long weekend or more in psychiatric care, but I resented him for bailing out. He was not supposed to let his emotions leak (as if they were blood or urine or vomit or meds) through the seams of his psyche. My father is selfish, I thought. All of us are hurting, but he gets to hold his hand up to get help for drowning, one, two, three.

Around the time my father banned my mother's parents from our home, my mother drew a cartoon and on a whim sent it in to the *New Yorker.* Mom read during her leisure time. A book always crowded her purse, cellophane-jacketed library books slid around like tiles in the backseat of her car. When she drew, she sketched rebuses and word games on her grocery lists: a chunk of glittering stone beside a pencil outline of a smiling cow for a "quartz" of milk, or a clucking hen to remind her to buy chicken. For her *New Yorker* submission she drew a single frame of an elevator in the lobby of an office building. A sign reading "Drug Treatment Center" hung over the elevator doors. She marked the elevator's call buttons "Uppers" and "Downers."

Mom and I were each privately fed up with my father's drug-addicted clientele and their traumas. We viewed their plights as decoys that helped my father fulfill his wish to implement justice in the world. With her pencil, my mother jabbed back at him.

My mother considered her parents fragile, even before her mother's anxieties emerged. Her father often said "your poor mama" about her mother for no reason that my mother knew, a phrase he began when my mother was young, and continued to the end of his life. My mother feared that not living up to her parents' dreams would break their hearts.

My mother stayed with my father throughout the worst of his depression. When we girls were small she was often happy; ours was a beautiful life, she remembers, and as Susie got sicker, and Sarah got sicker, and my father got stranger, she took pride—arrogance, she calls it now—in maintaining the illusion that nothing was amiss. To her, we were a smart and wonderful family. As daughters, Sarah and Susie and I were fun to be around. We were never boring, never disappointing.

My mother explains her life this way: "If a doorknob needed fixing, I could fix it with a screwdriver. If Susie got leukemia while I was dealing with Sarah, I could just deal with that, too."

She never confided in her parents beyond the most basic facts; she protected them from knowing for certain how far from shore her life had gone.

Our household ran better if Mom did everything herself. This was not entirely a symptom of sailing smoothly through Susie's and Sarah's and my father's overwhelming needs, or of keeping my life on an even keel. When she was a teenager, my mother took her blouses from her closet and reironed them after her mother had pressed them and put them away. "The creases weren't sharp enough," she remembers. Her brow furrows when she says this, still trying to keep her vanished Villager blouses neat.

My mother never got around to teaching me to separate clothes for the laundry or clean a bathtub, I think because she could see that I was easily distracted and impatient. She taught me other skills that surge in me like waves. She taught me to escort insects out the door instead of killing them. She taught me to adopt homeless dogs and cats. When I was a teenager and she taught me to drive in an empty parking lot in a boxy white car with a black vinyl roof, we circled around a Dumpster and I hit the brakes seconds before striking a matted and cowering collie. The dog came home with us, stinking up the backseat.

The vet called the geriatric dog a "retread," like an old tire with new grooves. My mother sent the dog to the groomer before she brought her home for a second round of life. She named the dog Charlie.

My mother was a member of her first generation of cousins to attend college. It occurs to me now that I am her only child to finish college.

When I was in college and for a decade after, my mother's letters to me were serious-minded pep talks, typed on office letterhead in italic font. They seem urgent to me now, the forward-leaning characters running and breathless.

She worried about my lack of confidence, my drift on the open ocean of my life. My habit of prefacing every statement with "I'm sorry." In her letters, she encouraged me. You are pretty, you are focused and smart, never fail to do that which makes you happy. Subtly encouraging me, she insisted that I was still there.

16.

Handler, Sarah E., age 27 years of Boston on August 13. Dear daughter of Miriam Handler of Boston & Jack Handler of Lee . . . Loving sister of Jessica A. Handler of Atlanta.

—*Boston Globe* obituary, Saturday, August 15, 1992

The day that Sarah died, she had called in sick to work. She had an office job at a manufacturing company, work that she was too smart for, but she enjoyed its camaraderie. The freedom of earning a paycheck buoyed her, as did the sense of purpose that came with autonomy. As for her health, her boss gave her time off when she needed it.

Pneumonia had dogged Sarah throughout her life, and on this day, she was only a few days out of the hospital. I imagine that her boyfriend had breakfast, kissed her goodbye, and left for work. Sarah read and watched television.

Her cats, Max and Toonces, napped on the blanket chest under the window.

Intuition tells me that sometime in the middle of the afternoon, Sarah swung her legs over the side of the bed and began to get up. Maybe she had to use the toilet, or maybe she felt like going into the kitchen for a snack. As she started to stand, whoever comes for us when we go arrived. The Grim Reaper. A cold wind. A white light. Sarah died quickly, falling back across her bed, with one arm behind her and the other by her side. Before she fell, I imagine her holding her hands up in surrender.

"I give," I hear her say. "Enough."

When her boyfriend came home that evening, the cats were serene: nothing they had seen that day flustered them. I imagine that, other than my sister's body across the covers, the bed was undisturbed. He called my mother at home.

"We're just sitting down to eat," she told him. "Can I call you back?"

"Mimi, it's bad," he told her.

My mother and her boyfriend, Joe, left the lights on and the dinner on the table. They drove the few blocks to Sarah's apartment. The ambulance and the medical examiner were already there. Sarah was pronounced dead at 6:38 PM.

• • •

The grief that comes from separating the living from the dead is acknowledged in a ritual at Jewish funerals, when mourners tear their garments or wear black ribbons cut in two.

At Sarah's funeral, the undertaker pinned ribbons to our chests before we left his office and walked into the chapel. A kind and efficient man whose services Mom and I had located in a matter of hours, he ripped one ribbon after another. The torn black grosgrain hung in two short strips. Ritually broken, we wore proof of our two-sided selves, living people then and now, before and after.

My mother and I sat in the funeral chapel's front row, my father and stepmother behind us. A bouquet of pink roses lay across the top of Sarah's pine casket, over the Star of David. I looked only once. For the remainder of the ceremony, I shifted my gaze from the wall to my lap. The flowers were a curiosity at a Jewish funeral. The candy-pink petals and long green stems made me catch my breath. As I did, Mom felt me stiffen.

She whispered, "I know we're not supposed to have flowers, but I couldn't not let her have them."

My mother and I sat rigidly, as if sound or movement would break us completely. At the rear of the chapel, a friend of Sarah's wailed, a sudden foghorn sound that tapered off into sobs. Listening to her moans, I envied her ability to mourn openly. I reached for my mother's hand.

Family and friends gathered at my mother's apartment for the shivah. I was very tired and my muscles were sore, as if someone had been pummeling me. Twenty-seven years of keeping watch, even from a distance, were over. I hadn't slept much. I had been at my mother's side since I arrived, as if my physical presence could keep her from breaking down.

Her living room was crowded and noisy; people sat thigh to thigh on the couch and two by two in armchairs. I shared an ottoman with someone before I moved to join a group in the dining room. Sitting in awkwardly close arrangements reassured us: the press of living bodies seemed to relieve pain. Deli trays and desserts were arranged on the table and coffee was brewing in the kitchen, but my stomach was tight.

My father and I did not talk much. There was such a great deal to say that we did not know where to begin. We sat together for a while, dumbstruck, before I excused myself to get some air.

When I returned, my father and stepmother stood by the front door, saying good-bye to friends. My stepmother had her purse over her shoulder, and my father had his hand on the doorknob.

I called out to my father over the steady hum of conversations and the insistent ringing phone. "Are you leaving?" I asked.

I was angry. Sarah had been dead less than two days. Her family and friends were inert with grief, and our father seemed to have other things to do.

He held up his hands, a gesture of surrender, and walked toward me. His actions pleaded, "Lower your voice. Let's not make a scene."

"I live far away," he said. "It's a long drive."

I walked toward him. I was ready to fight, for Sarah, for Mom, and for me, and unwilling this time to ignore my feelings. "It's three hours away, Dad."

My father shook his head, as if I didn't understand. Then he quoted the Robert Frost poem "Stopping by Woods on a Snowy Evening." Poetry would speak for him as always, beautiful language veiling excuses this time.

My mother had come into the foyer and stood behind me, her dislike of my father radiating like a force. I was no longer aware of my stepmother—only my mother, my father, and me, the remnants of a family.

My father's repeated turning from us enraged me. "Don't quote poems. Talk to me like I'm a real person. Your promises are here, to me."

My voice, as strong as his could be, gained power because I knew I was right. This must be the way an attorney feels when he's winning his closing argument, I thought. I kept going, without planning what I would say. "You still have a daughter. I'm still alive, and I want you to stay."

I was nauseated, shaking with anger and fear. I had never before spoken up to my father, certain he would respond with wrath or ridicule. I turned away, and he and my stepmother departed. Later, my mother told me how proud she was of me. When I confronted my father, she said, I had the stunned "I can do it" expression babies get when they take their first steps.

The baby steps I took on the day Sarah was buried were, in a way, unconscious. Wounded and confused, I knew that without Sarah the time had come to learn how to live without sisters. Mom and I had arranged Sarah's funeral, sat side by side across from her casket, and had returned home without her.

For the first time since my sisters' illnesses broke our family, I demanded justice for myself. I was thirty-two years old, and had been the well sibling since Sarah was born. The day of Sarah's funeral, I started to reclaim my own life.

A few days later, Mom and I sorted Sarah's belongings. We are practical people and needed something to occupy us. We wanted to check on Sarah's cats, and there were things we wanted to have.

Sarah's boyfriend, a pleasant guy we liked, may have been there when we packed and sorted, but I don't remember. Mom's boyfriend, Joe, a laconic Boston Irishman and union arbitrator, helped carry boxes downstairs to her car.

In the kitchen, I was cotton-headed. In the hall, my mother was inside a bubble. "Can you take these library books back?" floated distorted from her mouth; the words sounded like they came from a warped tape.

"Should I dump out the milk and yogurt?" I wondered.

Most of Sarah's clothes went into big black trash bags for Goodwill. She shopped almost exclusively at second-hand stores and taught me her secrets. Choose by touch. Run your fingers along the clothing on the rack and pull out the silks, the cashmeres, the linens, and cottons. Don't pick for color. Quality will last. At her biggest, my sister was two-thirds my size; quality would have to last for someone else.

Looking through her kitchen cabinets (because I wanted to live *for* her, and if I was going to live her life, I needed to know the intimate details about her home—where she kept her Tupperware, or if she needed to restock her paper napkins and cooking oil), I found an ashtray and an opened pack of Newports. A few months earlier, I had noticed her cigarettes on a table and presented them to her in high dudgeon. I had quit my own three-pack-a-day habit. I waved Sarah's cigarettes in her face.

She stared me down. "What difference," she asked, cool and aloof, "could it possibly make?"

I put the cigarettes back. Sarah had been right.

Here are some of the physical things I kept from Sarah's life:

- A lime-green T-shirt with a picture of Ronald Reagan's face bisected by a red slash.
- A pack of playing cards with pictures of Chippendales' male nude dancers on the back.
- A rubber-stamp kit with three colors of ink and a raised Cheshire cat face on a wooden block.
- A heavy brass container with the word Handler on the top in raised lettering: a military ammunition box. I bought the box at a flea market and gave it to Sarah because we liked to think that ours was an unusual surname. She polished the box with Brasso and used it on her desk for paper clips.
- An opened box of tampons.
- A *New Yorker* cartoon in which a man opens his door

to the Grim Reaper and muses about the poor timing: he had just gotten control of his life. I carry the cartoon in my wallet now, cautioning me the same way Sarah saw it: a reminder not to get too cocky.

I took the cartoon from under a magnet on Sarah's refrigerator and read the caption. Moving quickly, I folded the clipping in half across then half again down, and tucked it flat into my back pocket. This cartoon is something I have never shown my mother. When I peeled the clipping from where Sarah had put it, some version of "your poor Mama" swam in my mind. Despite what I had seen all my life, I believed that my mother was fragile.

My work or errands meant that I sometimes drove through a part of Atlanta that had been an undeveloped stretch of land when I was small. The neighborhood had lately been buried under a blistering concrete maze of strip malls and office parks. One road, I knew, led to the cemetery where Susie was buried. Every day that I passed that intersection I averted my eyes from the turn, ashamed that I had never visited Susie's grave.

Three years after Sarah died, I forced myself to make the right turn I had avoided. I drove for a few blocks, and then rolled through the gates and along the looped pathways of the cemetery, trying intuitively to locate where Susie's funeral had been. Topography and memory led me to the top of a hill, a high place at the eastern edge of the property. The population beneath my feet had grown in thirty years, but no marker verified the place where I was certain that Susie's body lay. There was only a mossy patch barely four feet long, a depression in the grass that had begun to sink with age.

At the cemetery office an assistant leafed through a record book, frowned, and buzzed an intercom to summon a supervisor. He sat me down in his office and said that I was correct, my sister was buried there, in the Garden of David, Section A. Exactly where memory, like a divining rod, had taken me.

I asked him why no headstone marked the grave.

Sadly, he said, no marker was ever bought or placed.

My urge was immediate: I asked him if I could buy a marker.

The funeral director shook his head and pushed a file across the desk to help make his point. Like real estate, a grave site is private property, he explained. My father owned it.

I nodded, sickened. Not one of us had been here since 1969.

My father and I had grown increasingly distant since I left Los Angeles. We had one another's mailing addresses. We exchanged birthday cards. He sent photos. At first, we heard the most basic news of one another's well-being through Sarah. He had left California, remarried, and moved to a town where western Massachusetts shoulders up against New York State. Sarah had been to visit, but when she died, I had not yet made the trip. After her funeral, I believed that I had little to bind me to my father.

"He only loves me when I am sick," Sarah once said to me.

I didn't disagree. I was rarely sick, and had never been really sick. My good health meant that I did not depend on my father in the way that had become usual in our family. My wellness must have been a kind of accidental belligerence, making me seem to him a traitor, a child able to get along without him.

Buying a headstone for Susie gave me a reason to confront him, but I didn't have my father's telephone number. Sarah, who would have been my first stop and my intermediary, was dead. It was up to me to be the big sister and confront my father alone. I could make one call to his home in Massachusetts and ask why he left this sad little grave unmarked, walking away from it on the day of the funeral and never coming back. I could insist that he remember Susie to the world, but I didn't. A call from me would have been perceived as a demand, my selfish cornering of a man who had had enough. In part, he would have been right. Asking him to have a headstone made for Susie would have been an appeal for him to look away from his own heartbreak and see mine.

There are families who visit their dead and sit beside a grave. If they are Jews, they place pebbles at the grave site as physical evidence of their remembrance. Otherwise, they rest a clutch of flowers or a framed photograph against the headstone, a gesture of love toward the lost.

In 1969, wrenched by one death and dreading another, my parents believed that making life full for Sarah and me prohibited backward glances. They did not visit Susie's grave, and I took their lead.

Instead of calling my father, I hesitated, and called my mother. I had not realized until I sat across the desk from the funeral director that Mom had never come back here. Telling her that Susie was buried in an unmarked grave would inflict a wound, but my need to right the inadvertent wrong done to my sister outweighed my urge to protect her.

My mother convinced the cemetery administrator that, as the property owner's wife (she did not tell them that she and my father had divorced), she could give permission for me to act on her behalf. Her name was not on the purchase agreement for the grave—only my father's.

"If there's any question about why," she told me, "it's because I was not present when the plot was purchased."

She had been at home with Sarah and me, and then at the funeral home, dressing Susie's body. My father's signature on the cemetery contract is an erratic line of stabbing motions, the frantic scrawl of a man undone.

About a week before Chanukah, I bought a simple bronze marker for Susie's grave. Two open hands, a Jewish symbol of benediction, spread over her name: "Susannah Jenny Handler, August 5, 1961–November 13, 1969."

17.

It almost seems shameful to me that I should have a care for my own life and well-being when many thousands of people have been wiped out with but a stroke or two.

—Excerpt from group e-mail from
Jack Handler, September 12, 2001

I had been back in Atlanta several years before my father and I began to circle one another again, establishing the beginnings of an uneasy truce. When my husband and I agreed to visit him at his home in western Massachusetts, Dad and I were tentative toward one another. With my father and stepmother, Mickey and I walked the wooded road near their house and admired their small town. I had been there with friends in college, while my father lived in Asia. Now, my father knew about the arts center in a famous nineteenth-century novelist's estate, and I knew about the old-fashioned soda fountain in the drugstore, where I used to wait for the Boston bus.

In his kitchen, my father boasted to me about his skill at cooking lamb. I reminded him that I had stopped eating red meat when I was eleven. All those years of barely talking left us unable to connect.

As we began to reacquaint ourselves, my father called me to tell me that he had been diagnosed with inoperable lung cancer. Forty years of smoking did not cause the cancer, he said. It must have been the time last winter when he slipped on black ice outside the root cellar and cracked his rib. He would try chemo for his wife's sake, but he and I both knew, he said, that there was no hope. He asked if I would visit him.

For the year that he lived, I flew to Massachusetts regularly to help look after my father. My stepmother took care of him daily, his sister came often from out of state for long visits, and his friends brought food, books, and movies on tape. When he moved from the upstairs bedroom to a hospital bed in his living room, he looked out on the front yard and the street. When he first got sick, I noticed that my wedding photograph hung in his study, one-third of a triptych with Sarah's high school yearbook photo, and a picture of Susie holding a snowball. After he died, I learned from his friends that he had bragged about me—my intelligence, my beauty, my career.

My father was very open about his illness. Medications and lab tests generated a language we knew how to speak.

He e-mailed his friends and family regularly about his experience, keeping us up-to-date with his chemotherapy, his dismay at losing his hair, and how he enjoyed the days he had energy. His e-mail messages about his cancer were often surprisingly intimate. Dad asked me to help him edit that correspondence into a piece for a local literary magazine. He had become a member of a writers' group. When he asked me to work with him, he did so as if he were proposing a business arrangement. I was honored to take on the task; asking me to help meant that my father saw me not only as an adult but as someone he could trust. In Massachusetts and in Atlanta, I read his correspondence again, and made only the smallest changes, talking them over with my father in his living room or on the phone long-distance. This final outing for us was, in a way, our lifeline.

When I told my father how sad I was that he had cancer and how wrong a turn of events his illness was, he equivocated. The worst that could happen already had, he said. I knew he meant losing Susie and Sarah. In my father's last year, we did not examine the ways in which our family had splintered, because we knew there was no turning back. My father was leaving for good, this time against his will.

While my father was sick, I was never afraid that the "it" that stalked my family would come for me. Although he was not old when he died—he had just turned sixty-seven—he was neither eight nor twenty-seven. The cause of his cancer was not a mystery. For these reasons, his death was a different kind of theft.

"This may be the last time we'll see each other in this corporeal world," I told my father a few weeks before he died. I knew he would appreciate the scholarly sound of *corporeal.* Dad sat in a recliner, an afghan over his shoulders, another in his lap. I crouched in front of him, leaning forward to feed him spoonfuls of soup.

My father's hands curled in his lap. His fingers were long and elegant, the tips yellowed by nicotine.

"I have your hands," I said, observing my long fingers above his. My father grimaced, drawing his hands back, Nosferatu-style, as if reclaiming them. I knew he was making a joke, teasing me the way he had when I was very small. Give me back my hands.

Earlier in his illness, my father one day said he wanted to talk to me. This made me nervous, stirring up teenage feelings of "What have I done now?" and a lifelong dread of hearing more bad news. I pulled a chair to his bedside, and heard him out. We did not want to fight. His request was simple. He asked me to forgive him. Looking him in the eye, I did.

I was at home the night my father died. My stepmother called me that evening, and put him on the phone with me. We knew that he was in the last few days of his life. I heard his labored breathing through the receiver, and could imagine him lying in his hospital bed in his living room, the macramé plant holder hanging from the ceiling in the corner, the chairs around him piled high with magazines, clothes, and medical paraphernalia. He said he loved me.

He was gasping. The words took effort, and I knew that he meant them.

I answered that I loved him, and offered the guidance he had given me years before, one day in the car when Sarah and Susie were alive and he and I were out on an adventure. "Don't be afraid."

. . .

Sarah and I never had a conversation about the "why" of Dad. We did not discuss whether he failed us, or what was wrong with him.

"He would smoke near an oxygen tent." We said this to each other more than once, shorthand for the way we saw his approach to the world. We envisioned Dad's cigarette, hanging bent and unlit from his lip in a hospital room. We imagined him striking a match, lighting up, and ignoring the "No Smoking" sign. Forgetting the plastic tent at the head of the bed with a child inside.

Blown to smithereens by our own father. It could happen.

"He's not nice to you," Sarah said, sometimes taking my side. Other times she defected. "You should treat Dad better," she said. "He loves you."

This made my throat tighten. She was right, I knew, but I didn't know how to treat him better, nor he me. When he lived in Singapore, Dad sent Sarah a three-foot-long Balinese marionette, with silk clothing and a severe wooden face. The arms and legs moved on sticks. In the same package, he sent me a mirror-spangled cotton vest sized for an eight-year-old. I was close to twenty. My father loved me, but he could not see me.

When Dad wasn't around, we joked about him. Cigarettes and the oxygen tent. Stuffing food in our faces with both hands. When he was nearby, we looked away. Dad yells at Sarah, I gaze at the ceiling. Dad yells at me, Sarah examines her nails. Dad storms out of the room because we are inconsiderate, ungrateful, and selfish. We fall over, laughing silently. Tension rises from us like steam.

When Sarah was in the hospital for long stretches, Dad sent gift boxes from Zabar's in New York or Happy Herman's in Atlanta. The idea of them made me wobble with guilt; there was no way to love our father enough to fill him. Inside the boxes, crazy with Excelsior, lay tins of smoked oysters, doll-sized jars of caviar, and hard white crackers from mills with quaint names. "Love, Dad," the card read. Sarah went through the contents of a box quickly if her mouth wasn't sore, doling caviar out to herself on a spoon and carefully arranging one smoked oyster per cracker, lining them up on paper towels to be eaten in neat rows.

Sometimes when the gift boxes came, like an assistance drop into a war zone, Sarah had been nauseated for days, and could not eat at all. She gave the gourmet food away at the nurses' station. A party for you guys; none for me. Where does a person keep her smoked oysters if she's in a hospital room? The plastic ice bucket? How long will they keep in the communal refrigerator in the parents' lounge before they gross out some family from the sticks?

Sarah and I did not discuss Dad, because in some ways we were just like him. We liked to be in the middle of the action. We collected the smallest bits of information so that we could be clever and trump someone else. *Per aspera ad astra*, from his cigarette pack. *Illegitimi non carborundum*. We know Latin, you don't, so we win.

When the credits rolled at the end of a television show, Dad liked to pretend he knew everyone there. "Bobby," he'd say, sounding chummy. "Good old Bobby. And Mary Jo. And Dick."

This came back to me when I was in my twenties and organizing the credit roll for a television show. As production coordinator, I typed the list of names for the control room. "Good old Bobby," I said. I had not planned to; the words just came out. "And Mary Jo. And Dick." My father, speaking through me, was in the room.

. . .

Before he died, I asked my father about Susie's death. I had wondered for years why he had told me that he and a mysterious someone had helped Susie die. What did they do, and why did she need it?

The morning that Susie died, my father sat beside me at our kitchen table. Speaking gently, more to himself than to me, he said that "they" had given Susie something to help her die.

Who are "they"? I wondered. What did "they" give her? I only nodded, unsure of what to say or do. My father told me never to tell my mother what he had just told me. On my calendar that day, I used the words that he and my mother used, and wrote "Susie dies peacefully" in the square for November 13.

Entrusted with what I thought was an adult secret that metastasized into an uneasy pact with my father, I said nothing for more than thirty years. My father and a mysterious someone, it seemed, had hastened Susie's death in some terrible final hour. Of course my father did not end my sister's life. I know now that he was speaking of a painkiller or sleeping pill that eased her discomfort, but he was not thinking clearly that night or morning. But by confiding in me and asking for my silence, he was building a wall between me and my mother. The question of what had happened when Susie died beat against my closed mouth like a pulse.

At his home in Massachusetts, my father pushed his chair back from his round wooden dining room table. He shrugged before he shuffled up the stairs toward the bedroom where I knew he would lie down, collapsing with a deep sigh. He had given up his lifelong habit of wearing suspenders—he called them braces—and I saw that his chinos sagged on his narrow hips.

"Understand me," I said to his back. "Why enlist my collaboration with a secret I did not understand?"

"Damaged," my father muttered from the stairwell. "You have to understand: I was damaged."

18.

A real laugh that I remember, a real temper, a real
kisser of cats.

—Journal, September 2004

The commuter train from Boston to Canton, Massachusetts, leaves South Station a few minutes after nine on
weekday mornings. I'm holding tickets for a trip I planned a
month ago, but I don't want to go. Taking the Attleboro line
to the suburbs south of Boston has been the hard pit lodged
in the center of our vacation.

This morning, I can't decide exactly where to stand on
the perimeter of the takeout café in South Station's lobby. I
want to order breakfast, but I can't catch the attendant's
eye. He pops up behind the toasters and then ducks down
again like a target in an arcade shooting gallery. When I finally get served, the coffee scalds my hand through the
foam cup and the bagel is cold and rubbery. Juggling the

food and a wad of paper napkins with our tickets and train schedule, I dart toward a filigreed metal table. This is a faux Parisian café, and I am faking sans souci, if only to myself. This will be an easy side trip, I promised Mickey. We'll be back by noon, plenty of time to go up Huntington Avenue and take in the Gardner Museum before closing time.

For twelve years, I have stayed away from Sarah's grave. My superficial reason is that I live in Atlanta and Sarah lived—and died—in Boston. My real reason is that I don't want to see the physical proof that her life is over. All I will see is a brass headstone facing skyward from the ground, but I have not reconciled myself to the severity of what it means.

I have been to London and Paris, Rio de Janeiro, and Guadalajara. I know the lyrics to nearly every Beatles song. I have soothed celebrity egos and squelched producer tantrums in Hollywood greenrooms. I can give a pill to a cat, and can thump a cantaloupe and make a good guess as to whether it's ripe. I can parallel park. I can sing harmony. I can make gazpacho. But losing the sister I knew best diminished me.

My husband, who never knew my sisters, welcomes their pictures and jokes and stories into our home. The first print from the woodcut that pressed ink into every one of the bookplates made in Susie's memory hangs, framed, in our hallway. Through Mickey, I was able to see myself again through the eyes of another person. With him, I was as ready as I would ever be to see Sarah's grave.

Inside the train car, the wood-grain Formica walls are dirty with food stains and years of scuff marks from shoes and snow boots. The fabric seats feel like scouring pads through my jeans, but they have a welcoming pretend-armchair look. The seats are as familiar as the threadbare lounge chairs from my freshman dorm. Being on a train—tossing my bag onto the overhead rack and breathing the ghost smells of stale cigarette air—thrills me unexpectedly; it's as if my body, not my mind, remembers the excitement of heading down to New York from Boston for long week-ends with my college roommates. The lulling sway as we pull away from Boston reminds me, too, of trips I didn't want to take, lugging my duffel bag and down jacket during winter break to Pennsylvania to visit Mom and Sarah and, before he left for Asia and then Los Angeles, to skirt my father's edges.

I slide down on my tailbone and pull my knees up, pressing them against the back of the seat in front of me. My feet dangle free. Triple-decker houses flicker past my window. It is a beautiful day. It's almost lapidary, this blue sky filled with the piercing, happy cheeping of birds.

At the cemetery office, we are given a map of the grounds. The woman at the front desk writes my name and Sarah's on a pad before she turns to a computer. The lobby is glossy-painted cinder block, like an elementary school cafeteria. Piled on a coffee table in front of a vinyl couch is a stack of cards printed with the Mourner's Kaddish—the Jewish prayer for the dead. Mickey pockets one.

The receptionist swivels back toward me, and smiles. She holds out two sheets of extralong copy paper hieroglyphed with lines and swirls and row upon row of neat little squares.

"Your sister is here, in Tekoah," she says, marking a section in yellow Hi-Liter. "Your grandparents are nearby, in Galilee."

She draws a yellow line from Tekoah to Galilee, across Shiloh and through Gilead. Releasing the maps into my hand, she reminds us not to place pebbles on the graves— the Jewish tradition showing that someone has come to visit a grave also wreaks havoc on lawn-care equipment. I thank her and drift out the door, feeling as though I am underwater, losing air.

Mickey and I walk the groomed concrete paths searching for Tekoah. We shade our eyes; we look right, and left, and then down at the map again. We are impostors, out for a stroll in a scrupulously manicured park. Give us binoculars and little vests, and we could pass for bird watchers. I never want to find my destination. I want to have arrived and left already so that a soft pad of time will have passed since I have looked at the grave.

I have been here only twice. The first was Sarah's funeral, the second, my grandmother's. After my grandmother's service, I sat in the backseat of the funeral-home limousine while it slipped through the cemetery and came to an idling stop at Sarah's grave. The sky was the gray of pencil lead, and a few inches of brittle snow glittered on the ground. Mom left the car and walked, rigid and glassy-eyed, to the graveside. Both of us would have done anything to have this place not be a part of our lives. I followed my mother out of the car. Standing tall and quiet, holding her hand, I saw myself instead down on my knees, clawing the snow and dirt with my bare hands.

Mickey and I find the section we are looking for almost by accident. Tekoah is on our right after we round a hill that looks just like all the other hills. What I have come for is just a few feet away, and I can no longer pretend that I am a bird watcher or a pedestrian, or that I am here for any reason but to see my sister's grave. I step out of my sandals and feel the grass, springy under my feet. I press my fingertips against the raised lettering on Sarah's headstone, warm in the sun, and then cool my fingers in the grass. For the time it takes for a breeze to blow, time shifts forward and back again. Someday I will exist only in someone's memory. I want to jam my thumb into my mouth, or curl up tight and hard, like a gray pill bug. I feel cocooned and quiet, and am a little embarrassed by my primitive urge to rock back and forth.

Behind me, Mickey has the card from the office in his hand. I don't know the words to the prayer, and he needs to read along to prompt his rusty Hebrew, but he begins the Mourner's Kaddish. *Yitgadal v'yitkadash sh'may raba* . . . Chiming in the few intermittent words I know—*yisrael, amen*—calms me. The prayer gives thanks for life, never mentioning death. Perhaps I am doing something good for my sister, perhaps for myself. You never know. *Amen.*

Mickey and I say the concluding words at the same time. We have ignored the rules and gathered pebbles on our walk through the cemetery, which we place beside Sarah's name. I lean my face against my husband's shirt and smell his cologne. I feel his heart beat in his warm chest.

Tekoah is named for the birthplace of a Hebrew prophet named Amos, who instructed people to let justice rain down like water. It was also the name of a skinny yellow tomcat, one of the succession of cats Sarah adopted and loved in her lifetime. Sarah once cut an ad for a greasy spoon called "Amos's Restaurant" out of a coupon flyer stuffed in her front door. Hash brown and egg special Sunday mornings. Free coffee refills. Homemade pie. She taped the clipping onto the pantry drawer where she kept the cat food.

Sarah lived every day knowing that her body would fail. Even in her teens, she knew intuitively that her natural death would come before mine or our parents'. Someday there would be an infection from which she could not recover.

Although we never spoke about Susie, Sarah must have been haunted by the fact that her next-oldest sister had already died. She never told me if knowing the likely circumstances of her death made her afraid, or angry, or sad. I never wanted to ask. Kostmann's Syndrome was our conversational equivalent of Tolstoy's white bear.

Casually discussing illness and how it had changed each of us, approaching the idea with words other than the picketed, formal language of medications and diagnoses, was to give it a place in our home and accept it into the family. The fact that Sarah's illness was already there, sometimes in the corner, sometimes filling the room, went without comment. My parents set the example of an overriding sense of decorum and privacy. Illness was the bear in the corner we tried not to think about, but could never completely ignore. Illness was the wind at the gate. Our silence held the gate shut.

Even though I have outlived them, I remain responsible, in a way, for the stories of my sisters' lives. Our mother remembers different parts of their days than I do. She remembers their births, their babyhoods. She remembers the Halloween costume she made for Susie from a cardboard crate, construction paper, and white tights. As a pack of L&M cigarettes, Susie made her way around the neighborhood through eyeholes in the cardboard and cleaned up in the Mars Bar department. Dressed as a devil that same night, my sole desire was possession of a real pitchfork, which we didn't actually own.

Sarah was in elementary school when I was in high school, in high school when I was in college. When she wrote me letters, she signed them "Love and other indoor sports," a giggly phrase from a novel she had read, a reference to a little girl's idea of sex. When Sarah was in high school, Mom came home from work one afternoon to find Sarah red-eyed, nodding yes into the phone, crying too hard to speak. Our father was on the line. Sarah, he said, was a parasite—greedy and selfish. He had no money, and if she would come see him in Los Angeles she would know just how hard it was: he had been living in his car. If Sarah loved him, now was the time for her to prove it. He could not pay child support. He could barely afford to feed himself. "Tell your mother," he said, "to stop bleeding me." Mom snatched the phone from Sarah's hand. Go to hell, she swore, before hanging up. She would take care of Sarah, and me, on her own.

Living in that two-bedroom apartment, Mom put aside two hundred dollars so that Sarah could get the cheap paint job she wanted for her first car, a used rust bucket. I had already left home.

· · ·

My mother's parents are buried side by side in an older, shadier section of the cemetery. My grandfather died in his sixties of a heart attack. My grandmother lived twenty years more, until her heart failed. Having no more stones to leave, I place a butterscotch candy next to my grandfather's name, and a mint beside my grandmother's. I chatted with them. You never know. I introduced Mickey; he said hello.

It was reassuring to be near the last physical place of the people I love. The middle initial of my grandmother's name stands for her maiden name, Braunstein. The birth date on my grandfather's headstone marks a day in Russia in 1904, before the revolution, in a town on the eastern length of the Trans-Siberian railroad. People cease to live, and the information that adds up to equal the facts of their lives goes missing as fewer of us stand here, above ground.

The cabbie who drove us back to the train station was a chatty man with a sagging face and wiry black hair. He looked like my Russian grandfather. When he speaks, it's with a vaguely eastern European accent, the sharp consonants washed to softness like the starch in hard-worn blue jeans. In the backseat of his cab, I dig through my purse for the train schedule and my wallet. Mickey rests his hand on my thigh, keeping me rooted in the living. I have already put on my sunglasses, hiding my emotion.

But our cabbie had driven this route before, and saw right through me. "It's almost *Yizkor*," he says gently. Yom Kippur is a month away. Even as an unobservant Jew, I cleave to the High Holy Days of the Jewish New Year, the days to consider beginnings and endings. On Rosh Hashanah, we ask to be written in God's Book of Life. Ten days later, on Yom Kippur, we ask God to take into account the souls of our loved ones. "It's good to remember," the cabbie says, almost casually, as he drives us slowly out of the gates and onto the main road into town.

19.

Yesterday, we got our marriage license . . . I did not
change my name . . . I have a name already.

—Journal, April 1998

Mickey and I traded family stories on our second date, over
draft beer and the clatter of pool balls in a bar.

"I want to tell you something kind of weird about me,"
he began.

"Try me," I challenged.

He took a deep breath. "I have a grown daughter who I
haven't seen since she was thirteen. When I was sixteen, I
got a girl pregnant. I was stupid and didn't use a condom.
Her parents convinced her to keep the baby. I wanted to get
away from what I had done, so I faked my own suicide and
ran away from home."

Mickey had been a junior in high school. He left his
jacket as a decoy on a bridge over the Tennessee River, and

a note that read, "Because I can't provide for my future child, I have chosen to end my life." A middle-class boy, son of a dentist, he assumed that there would be a life insurance policy that could help raise the baby.

Because he liked comic books and had a talent for sketching, Mickey thought it might be a good idea to earn his living as a street artist in New Orleans, a place he had seen only on television. He rode a Trailways bus all night from his home in Chattanooga to New Orleans. When the police brought the suicide note to his parents, they had the river dragged. The rescue squad found a dog's skeleton and some crushed beer cans. Mickey's grandparents came to his parents' house as if they were sitting shivah. He might not be dead. He could eventually show up or call home.

Four hundred and fifty miles away, Mickey reveled in his new life as a man on the run. He spent his days roaming the city. He drew pictures. He saw a matinee of *The Exorcist* and let himself get scared. He spent nights on a cot in a homeless men's shelter. Someone there told him he could pick up a day's work as a roustabout on an oil platform in the Gulf of Mexico. Because he was six feet tall and as broad-shouldered as a linebacker, he got the job. He didn't call home for two weeks.

The way to get a hot meal and a clean cot, if you were a vagabond in New Orleans in 1974, was to get arrested. One way to get arrested was to sleep outdoors in a tourist area. When Mickey decided to go home, he intended to go as a wanted man. He lay down to sleep on a sidewalk in the French Quarter. Before sunrise, he was arrested for vagrancy. What Mickey learned watching detective shows on television proved true. The incarcerated get one phone call. Mickey called home.

Mickey's father flew to Louisiana and bailed him out. They didn't go directly home to the ranch house on the cul-de-sac. Instead, Mickey and his father joined his mother, two brothers, and sister partway through their summer vacation. Direct from a New Orleans drunk tank, Mickey's dad delivered him to Opryland.

Mickey had limited contact with his daughter and the girl he had dated. He eventually stopped seeing them completely. It was a relationship that he felt he couldn't maintain, and he decided that erasing himself from their lives would be best for everyone involved.

For once, it was my turn to hold still, to show no reaction. He was telling the truth. Until that night, Mickey was simply a man I knew casually from work, another producer from another department at the enormous cable network that employed us. We said "Good morning" in the hallway before he went off to where the comedy writers were, and I took the elevator to the fourth floor, where I worked as a production manager for the documentary department. He was tall and soft-spoken. He wore cardigan sweaters when the weather cooled, ignoring the trends followed by his goateed colleagues in their vintage T-shirts and baggy shorts. Once, when we crossed paths in the parking garage, he helped me lift a heavy box of videotapes into my car. Later, when he asked me out for a beer, I said no. When he asked again, I said yes.

"So, what about you?" Mickey asked. "Tell me about where you grew up, what it was like."

Here's where he gets up and runs, I thought, taking a sip of my beer. "I am the oldest of three girls, and I am the only one still alive," I said, beginning the story pried out of me with every new friendship and every date.

I had learned to watch my listener's reactions while I told my story. Did my date look away from me and scrutinize the dusty plastic St. Pauli Girl sign over the bar? Would he tell me that he knew an old lady once who "caught cancer," or that he understood how I felt because his dog had died?

How a potential lover reacted to my story predicted the way he would behave toward me. Talking about death is like admitting you have wet yourself. Death is embarrassing: a failure. Death is indecent. My being acquainted with the aftermath of death, especially the deaths of a child and a young woman, made me somewhat of a Cassandra.

I have read that because so few people have been to the moon, astronauts have found that they can fully connect emotionally only with other astronauts. When I finished telling my tale at the bar, the man who would become my husband looked me in the eye. Each of us recognized that we had been to the moon.

. • .

The year that I decided to return to Atlanta to live, my paternal grandfather died, leaving money for my father, me, and Sarah.

With my share, I bought a house, a brick bungalow then nearly seventy years old, in an Atlanta neighborhood that reminded me of the one where I grew up. Like my childhood home, it had a steep, wooded front lawn, and a long driveway that wound out of sight from the street. Unlike the home that I still walked through in my dreams, boxcars at the freight yard two miles north of my new home clanged and screeched at midnight when they were uncoupled in the switching yard. A few blocks east of my house, on Sunday afternoons outside the storefront Holiness Church, black women in white gowns and hats like peaked meringues chatted and rippled the air with paper fans before they drove away in heavy, candy-colored Cadillacs.

I moved into my own small house two months before my thirty-first birthday. I bought the house from an elderly widow. She wanted to sell because she could no longer see well enough to maintain the sizable garden in the backyard. Because I moved in on a Sunday, the electricity had not yet been switched over to my name, and the movers wouldn't bring my furniture until the next day. I slept the first night in a sleeping bag on the bare living room floor. No curtains hung in the windows to block the haze from the streetlights. Cave crickets fluttered like dry leaves in the empty fireplace. I needed a flashlight to illuminate my path down the narrow hall to the bathroom. I didn't care. I was ecstatic.

My maternal grandmother sent a mezuzah as a housewarming gift, painted green and gold like a peacock's tail. My father had once put a silver mezuzah beside the front door in our old house, but since we rarely used that door, I stopped noticing the cigarette-sized blessing scroll after he installed it. In my own home, I went down to the basement for a hammer and box of nails. Feeling timeless and strangely happy, I banged my mezuzah's wooden shell to the front door frame.

For the next three years, my house lived beneath my hands and in the muscles of my back, under my nails, and in my lungs.

Excited and eager to show off the house, I invited Sarah down. I wanted my sister to be as thrilled about my house as I was.

Sarah declined the offer. Maybe I'll come in a few months, she said. When a few months had passed, she said maybe later. She did not mention what I think now must have been on her mind: that my investing in a house laid claim to the square one we both wanted. Perhaps Sarah, who had trained herself to keep quiet about the injustice born in her, chose to sidestep what was not yet obvious to me: that buying a home presumes a long and stable view of life. Why go see your house and hear your plans for the future? she must have thought. Let me enjoy the life I've made while I have it.

I know I said the self-satisfied things that new home-owners say, calling the house "my retirement fund," and reminding friends who raised their eyebrows at the junked orange Honda in the backyard adjoining mine that my worn-down neighborhood will only get better. Just think, I said, what my house will be worth in ten years.

Prying ancient carpet tacks from my floor with the claw of a hammer, I settled into a home of my own. My childhood, adolescence, and young womanhood were behind me. Sarah had become an adult despite the odds. Susie was dead. My father was, for the moment, absent from my daily life. On her own, my mother had bloomed.

Sarah bought a new car with her share of our grandfather's gift, after researching the data on every make and model she liked. The rest of the money she put in the bank. She sent photos to me of her and her boyfriend at dinner, Sarah in a sexy black dress and high heels. Her fair skin glowed against the black.

I phoned to ask about the evening.

"We ate gnocchi," she said. "I didn't know you're supposed to pronounce that 'nookie.'"

On each end of the phone line, we snorted at the sexual slang.

"Someone on my street has roosters," I said. "And a donkey. I hear it braying. Roosters crow all the damn time, not just at dawn."

Be careful, Sarah teased. Stay away from that yard. Your neighbors might be into voodoo. Some night they'll sacrifice the birds, then ride the donkey over and get you.

When Sarah died, I had been in my house just over a year. Her unspent cash went to me, according to the provisions of our grandfather's will.

"Here," I imagined her saying, a word delivered with a shrug. "Here, take this, I'm not using it."

Sarah and Jessica grown up

This money could not go toward the frivolous, a new car or a vacation. Instead, I pursued the resolutely practical, having a new roof put on the house and modernizing the plumbing: rusting iron pipes replaced with copper and PVC. With my hands in leather work gloves, I ripped strips of red and black linoleum and layers of dark pitch from the hallway floor, and was rewarded by the sight of bourbon-colored planks of heart pine. I pried open window sashes so tight they felt as if they had been painted shut during the Truman administration. I hired painters to cover the swimming pool–blue concrete front steps with a sedate color called "Dolphin Gray," and I painted pastel colors on every interior wall of the house. Friends helped out on weekends, and romances began and ended with projects. One boyfriend taught me to use a tile cutter, another had a circular saw, yet another could rewire the fuse box. Few stayed over, and often, after we went out for beer or dropped by a party, I was glad to head home alone. I wanted my house to myself.

Almost all my life, I believed that my responsibility was to protect other people, but once I had my own home I chafed at other people's troubles. Minor eddies that would have once captured my attention became unwelcome intrusions; I was annoyed when a boss called me at home from London on my day off so that I could help her remember a phone number, when a traveling boyfriend tried to make my couch his temporary home, or when a scold of scallop-edged invitations to baby showers for women I barely knew arrived in the mail or my in-box at work. I had only begun to catch brief, clear glimpses of myself. Distractions could easily make me forget how to see inside. Instinct told me to keep my head above water and watch for the shore.

I lived alone, looking for myself, for five years.

Mickey and I moved in together after a year of weekend migrations from my house to his apartment and back again. I wanted to live with Mickey, but I could not give up my house. We went from dating to being a couple in a matter of months.

"I wonder what inspires Mickey to love me," I wrote in my journal. I wondered how someone would be willing to overlook my serrated edges and my sullen silences the way Mickey could.

When I stayed nights at Mickey's apartment, he got up at dawn to walk a fast few miles, a baseball cap pulled down tightly over his curly hair, his bearded chin tucked into the neck of his sweatshirt. He left the coffee on and closed the apartment door gently, leaving me undisturbed to roll over and go back to sleep. I burrowed under his covers and slept until he came home. Once, asleep at his place, I dreamed that my childhood home had grown a second story. Assessing the new roofline from the street, even in my sleep I knew that the addition was Mickey.

While we dated, Mickey watched me with his nieces. With a little girl's warm hand in mine again, I was twinned and torn. The middle niece sat beside me on her grandparents' couch and showed me a picture she had drawn at school. Together, we identified a dog and a flower, and we sounded out the block letters of her name staggering across the top of the page. We shook glitter from the blobs of glue that pimpled the drawing, and laughed when the sparkles alighted on her skin, but a mirror-me screamed silently. The cry of "Unfair!" that I fought after Susie died rang in my ears. Playing with a child, I struggled to conquer my envious thoughts. What right, I thought, do you have to be a little girl? How long will you live, and who will be damaged if you die? I wondered. I could not escape my fears, even in the presence of healthy little girls unaware of my past.

One night, Mickey and I met up with two of his siblings and their children for pizza. One had grown to be a little girl who wore her baseball caps backward and opened her eyes wide just before she laughed. At the table, she made a wisecrack that came and went, but the way she spoke jolted me. She sounded like Susie. I excused myself and moved quickly to the ladies' room, where I gagged at the sink. I had not heard Susie's voice in thirty-six years.

These girls resemble my husband in slight and indelible ways: wavy hair, easy motion, quick wit. Were Mickey and I to have children, I think they would look a little like their cousins.

When Mickey proposed to me, my mind slowed and then stuttered to a complete stop. I had never once envisioned myself as a bride. What would happen if I say no? I wondered. Embracing a life that conventional wisdom dictates is bound to happen couldn't possibly happen to me. I am loss, not gain.

Mickey proposed in earnest, but I worried that this, too, would go badly because everything good eventually does. My thinking this way is a habit and a talisman, an invocation of the Yiddish *keynehora* to ward away the evil eye, a gesture of safety I believe in even as I close my eyes and kiss my fiancé. Before I kiss him, I do not say no. I say yes. Hearing my voice, I am surprised, although I have no doubt that I want to marry him. Where did this faith in my future come from? For an instant, I wonder if there is some hidden me pushing the word *yes* from my lips.

The next day I asked Mickey if he had meant what he said. Ask me again, I say, teasing him. Ask me when we are doing something mundane, because that is how we will live out our lives if we are lucky. When I am emptying the dishwasher, ask me, or when you are grinding open a can of food for the two gray tabbies snaking around your ankles.

Mickey wants a baby with me, a second chance at fatherhood. Because I want to please him, I hew to the edge of agreeing. Maybe with Mickey beside me I could put my fear aside and become a parent. Mickey's fears about parenting were different from my own. He had told me a family story about a long-ago uncle with a tumor discovered to be a parasitic twin. We laughed, but that hairy, toothy ball of not-child seemed to both of us a sinister warning. Genes, we know, have long memories.

Because we are each past thirty-five when we begin our relationship, we know that time is short for my safe pregnancy. We discuss names. Mickey wants Ben for a boy, after an uncle. I like the name Ben. I could have been a Ben. I cannot fathom naming a child Susie or Sarah. I cannot imagine calling those names in my house or yard and having anyone but my sisters respond. I suggest Josephine instead, in honor of my mother's mother.

We make our appointment with the Genetics Department at Emory University, the same hospital system that once cared so well for my sisters. If we had a baby, would our baby have Kostmann's Syndrome? Maybe, says the geneticist.

Possibly. At this time there is no reliable carrier testing. Both of your parents carrying the gene means there's a 67 percent chance of your being a carrier. If you went ahead and got pregnant, we could test the placenta, insert a needle through your abdomen. This is a standard way we test for genetic defects in a fetus.

Mickey and I grip hands. Needles haven't made me flinch since I was eight years old. What, though, would we do when the test is complete and the results come back with the news that I know in my bones will surface? No gambling spirit lives in me. Sixty-seven percent in me and none in Mickey is still more of a risk than I can take.

The presence of one seriously ill child in a family can obliterate a marriage. Two is unthinkable. The emptiness that comes with losing a child flattens almost any parent. Two people who were well matched at the beginning come apart because one grieves openly and the other silently, or one arranges the pill bottles on the shelf alphabetically and the other by dosage strength or time of day taken. One parent believes that the three o'clock medication has to go down his daughter's throat no later than five minutes after three, while the other parent says the hell with it, she's feeling well today and wants to go play with her friends, put the afternoon pills with the dinner pills.

When there was not enough money to cover the obscene expenses, my father turned to his parents. I know this now, but sensed it at the time, because I "helped" my father pay the bills. My job was to punch numbers into the adding machine as he called them out to me. He said two numbers, I answered back one, and he wrote with a pen into a hard-bound ledger. Most times he globbed over the number with correction fluid and made me repeat the math. The numbers could not possibly be right. He chain-smoked and swore, and I could not put my finger on exactly what was wrong this time. Maybe it was the numbers. Maybe it was me.

Dad called out, although I was barely two feet away, "Five dollars and twenty-seven cents plus one thousand dollars and no cents."

"Dad, did you say 'twenty cents'?"

"Goddamn it, now I have to find that bill again." He ground a Pall Mall into the abalone-shell ashtray.

At the time, I had no concept of what my sisters' medical care, plus my father's pills, our school clothes, books, groceries, vacations, and birthday presents cost. No one said no to us, and rarely did something cost too much. Dad went regularly to conferences and union meetings out of state, and later traveled to other cities interviewing for jobs. Sarah and one or both parents flew to New York or Boston on short notice for portions of her medical care. We flew to Pennsylvania and New York to see relatives, and later, Sarah and I went to Florida for winter vacations with our paternal grandparents. We were not a family who drove long distances. Planes were efficient, and we did everything in a hurry.

This is profligate, Mom said, when Dad took her to a resort hotel in the mountains. We need this money for other things. My father told her to stop grousing, and ordered from the top of the menu. He insisted on the best of everything to make himself feel better, and to force us to remember that the good life was ours.

There is good in our lives now, Mom insisted. Sarah and Jessica are good and smart and pretty. There are days—months—when Sarah is not laid low in the hospital. My mother saw the proverbial glass as half-full. My father saw the glass as not big enough, not the right glass.

When he didn't work because he had been let go for berating employees during midnight phone calls, because his law practice needed clients, or because the drug treatment center had closed, checks came in from his parents. Our family medical expenses were immense. His income, along with Mom's, and the health insurance that they never let lapse often did not cover costs. Every check my father deposited that he did not earn, and every medical bill he paid, was an indictment of his ability to be a father and a husband. My father was ashamed, and he took it out as anger.

In families, so much love and concern go toward the child or children who need the most that attention is spread inequitably among those who need less. A fatally ill child becomes the wrecking ball that destroys a home.

My husband is, in the end, more important to me than a baby. Mickey sees in my smile the face I had when I was six years old, before my sisters began to die. He has seen this face in photographs, and he says he is happiest when he can make me smile like I used to—guileless and unafraid.

Mickey is patient with me. He tells me the truth. I do the same for him. I know that he would have made a terrific father. I would have been a good mother. My sisters would have liked Mickey, thought him good-looking, and good enough for me.

Sarah and I called the wedding pages of the Sunday *New York Times* the "women's sports section." It seemed to us that the paper reported on weddings that were almost exclusively society affairs, euphoric descriptions of floral arrangements, string quartets, and one blissful couple after another attended by battalions of flower girls, groomsmen, and maids of honor.

"Listen to this one," I would crow before I dropped my voice to an approximation of a plummy British butler's accent.

Sarah countered with unfortunately hyphenated surnames. The idea of a woman named Kent and a man named Cook creating a bride saddled with the fatalistic surname "Can't-Cook" became a family joke.

Passing newsprint pages back and forth across the kitchen table, we had our own reasons for deriding frivolous and unenlightened womanhood. I insisted I would never dress in white and become someone's wife. Sarah knew she wouldn't.

When Mickey and I discussed our wedding plans with my mother, she suggested that we elope. "Save the money," she said. "Invest what a wedding would cost, and go get married by a justice of the peace."

My family no longer had a lexicon for happiness or normalcy. We were practiced in funerals, but weddings were the anomaly. Thinking back then over the history of my immediate family, I realized that I had been to exactly two weddings: a cousin's ceremony at a restaurant in Manhattan more than twenty years before, and my aunt's wedding, when Susie and I were small.

"I want to do something happy for this family," I told my mother. "I want to change our luck."

My mother was wildly excited. She helped me pick my dress—white as a cake, lacy as a doily, so ridiculously not the me I knew that I laughed out loud the first time I tried the dress on. When I modeled it for her at home, standing on a bedsheet on the floor so that the white crepe train wouldn't collect cat hair, she got teary-eyed.

I ordered wedding invitations. Mickey and I registered at department stores, the kinds of places we never shopped. We got at least three seder plates as gifts. We were given the things that set the table of normal life.

For several months after Mickey and I decided to marry, I was tormented by dreams in which Sarah and Susie tried on flower girl dresses and white gloves, comparing colors and sizes, zipping up one another's dresses, and smoothing each other's hair. Had they been living, Sarah would have been thirty-three, Susie thirty-six. They would be grown women, perhaps with husbands and children.

Mickey's parents were puzzled by our vision of a wedding. We had already declined to be married in their synagogue. We wanted to get married outdoors under the blue spring sky. We didn't want to leave Atlanta for our wedding. Hating the idea of "giving myself away," I would walk myself down the aisle alone. I would also be married without bridesmaids.

"Why won't you have any bridesmaids?" Mickey's mother asked.

Bridesmaids should flank my steps before they moved aside like curtains at my entrance to the huppah—the wedding canopy.

"I will have bridesmaids," I said, knowing that I sounded strange, and sure that I didn't care.

"My sisters will be beside me," I explained. "Only I will see them."

Mickey and I got married in the beginning of May 1998, at a historic building in Atlanta. It was the kind of sparkling southern spring day that gets written up in guidebooks. That morning we made coffee and danced in our underwear in the kitchen to ska hits, played loud. My house had become our house the year before. We brought Mickey's furniture, his comic book collection in orderly cardboard boxes, a new washer and dryer. My small house felt smaller, but it also felt right. After one tense afternoon of circling each other like edgy dogs, we relaxed.

For our wedding, Mickey ordered white satin yarmulkes in quantity from a supplier in New York, and had a rubber stamp made. A few weeks before our wedding, we spent an evening sitting across from each other on the floor, leaning on our living room coffee table and pressing the words "Place Head Here" inside one hundred yarmulkes.

"Some people might appreciate the instructions," Mickey explained.

In the garden behind the reception hall, Mickey and the rabbi waited under a huppah that my childhood friends

Mary Beth and Eleanor had made from branches of privet hedge intertwined with ribbons.

My father and stepmother sat near my mother. I had invited them, and at first, my father was reluctant. He wrote back a formal reply, asking what his role would be.

Come to my wedding and have a good time, I answered. I did not add what I was thinking: Please don't spoil this. Please don't make this about what is missing from our lives.

He came because my stepmother insisted, and because my mother was angry enough to call him. It was the first time they had spoken since Sarah's funeral. There are no obligations, she said. Just show up.

While the rabbi spoke, Mickey and I held hands, our fingers cold from nervousness. Mickey stomped on a glass; friends and family shouted, "Mazel tov!" We did not look like people who had holes in their hearts.

The salmon and roasted vegetables and bread and cheeses were excellent, and so were the wine and iced tea and lemonade and strawberries in chocolate. The jazz quartet played standards and sang swing tunes. My mother made a toast, and so did Mickey's father. My uncle played what he called "a musical toast," a clarinet solo of the first verse and chorus of "Sunrise, Sunset."

Mickey and I danced to "At Last," not caring that it was a little off-key. When I danced with my father, I thought of how I had stood on the tops of his feet when I was very small, holding his hands as he shifted back and forth. This was the first time since then that I had danced with him.

Almost everyone got up to dance the hora. I held hands with my cousins and party guests and husband and parents and in-laws, winding and kicking in a circle from table to table. I swung my hips and tried not to confuse which foot kicked forward when. An image of myself at five, leading Susie through a pretend-Indian dance in our Detroit back-yard filled my mind. Instead of shaking my head to dislodge this memory of my childhood, I welcomed it. The band played "Hava Nagila"—"Rejoice and Be Glad." Someone pulled me into a chair, and a surge of hands lifted me up. I clung to the armrests and shrieked, swaying in midair. If I looked down, would I see Sarah in the laughing crowd below?

When the sea of hands returned me to the floor, Mickey's friends and family lifted him skyward and jounced him up and down. He laughed and waved his arms above his head. When he came down, he was pale, but happy. Our knees were shaking, but we were back on solid ground.

20.

Today was—is?—Sarah's birthday.

—Journal, January 4, 1996

Once when I was in college, Sarah and I went for a walk on the shore at Singing Beach, north of Boston. We had come to see an architectural sand-castle contest: countless mermaids, a Great Wall of China lapped by the sea, and a silty dragon as big as a couch. We tossed the crusts of our sandwiches to seagulls.

"You know, they will explode if they eat an Alka-Seltzer," Sarah said.

We shuddered and giggled at the idea of guts raining from the sky.

A little more than a decade later that day came back to me in a dream. Sarah walked with me for a few steps before she turned away from the beach and swam out to sea. She was not a swimmer in waking life: seawater and pool water were too alive with bacteria for her immune system. My dream self, anxious, called out to her to be careful. Please come back. She swam farther out in the gray sea, and I knew that she had gone too far to hear me.

A voice whispered in my ear, telling me to let her go, that she knew what she was doing. I woke up weighted with awe, and called Sarah to tell her my dream. Sleepy, I dialed the wrong number, and then apologized to the stranger on the line. I didn't try again. Sarah would be on her way to work, I reasoned, no time to chat with me about my dreams.

On the first night of Chanukah, 1967, when Susie and I matched each other as ardent readers, our parents gave us a children's calendar to share, wacky pages with stickers commemorating "Great Day!" and "Too Much Homework!" Each year, we looked forward to the calendars' frantic illustrated cultural trivia in cartoon form—Giuseppe Verdi in a white wig indicating his birth date in quarter notes, Stanley and Livingston, in pith helmets, meeting at Victoria Falls. On one page, Susie drew a grinning figure with a tail unfurling from a lusciously curved rear end. I sketched hippies, skinny bearded men holding up two fingers in the peace sign. We were good and earnest girls. We took the quiz pages of our calendars as seriously as we did school. For "Best Game" we agreed on Twister. Our "Best TV Personality" was the Beatles. In the address section, next to the questions "Solar System" and "Galaxy" we wrote, "Yes."

A date book of my mother's from that time takes everything at face value: a teeth cleaning for me, a chemotherapy appointment for Susie, and a trip to a specialist in New York for Sarah. The dog goes to the vet, I go to ballet class, and Dad goes to a baseball game. Mom and Dad go out to dinner—call the babysitter. Looking at those pages now, I am stunned by my parents' will to keep our lives marching forward, making our childhoods as normal as they could be.

What does it mean to be the last one standing? On a day when I was trying to determine the driving time between two cities, I found a Web site that calculates the time passed between any two dates. I chastised myself as I clicked through to the questionnaire. Why did I want to see these facts? I know that a life is more than accrued time. My fingers galloped ahead of my brain, and typed in Susie's birth date on one line, the date of her death on the other. The computer did the figuring. Having gone this far, I typed in Sarah's statistics. Without knowing their laughs or their smiles, my computer did the equations. Sarah lived 10,083 days. Susie lived 3,022. The numbers mean little until they are used as comparisons: with more than 17,000 days behind me, I am still here.

My interior life and memory feel suspect without sisters. Did a friend of our father's, campaigning for city hall or the U.S. Senate, pluck Susie from a crowd at a parade and hold her high in his slow convertible, or was it Sarah? My sisters would remember the sunshine, the streamers, the applause that have grown hazy to me. Didn't we have a babysitter who once shepherded us, dressed in our flannel nightgowns and pajamas, still sluggish from sleep, into the overbright kitchen before arming each of us with sharp steak knives? Whispering instructions, didn't she arrange us by height, with me, the tallest, in the lead, and then follow us around our dark front yard to stalk the source of a scraping sound that only she heard? Susie and Sarah, who followed me that night in careful steps, would remember.

My old sticker calendars gradually acquired the same mystery as the ruins of Pompeii. They were moments of beautiful life captured accidentally just before all hell broke loose. After thirty-five years, I surrendered to my curiosity and pried the calendars loose from the bottom of a carton, moving aside yolk-colored boxes of 35-millimeter slides that held pictures of three sisters at a zoo, on swings, held in laps. Three transparent girls.

On a psychedelically decorated page beside the question "Intended occupation when grown up," I had written, "Mother." My childhood ambition might as well have giggled and waved. My own hand could not have written that. This must have been the dream of some other child from some other family. Still, I saw myself at nine years old, sprawled on my stomach on the tile floor of our den. In my right hand I clutched a blue ballpoint pen, in my left I dangled a spoon over a dish of ice cream. I stuck the tip of my tongue between my lips to help myself concentrate on keeping my writing on the lines.

"I want to be a mother, too," Susie said, reaching into our cigar box for a colored pen. She flopped down beside me and nudged my arm off the page.

I can't imagine being a mother now. A cough is never a cold when I think of Sarah. Feeling tired is more than what happens if you stay up past your bedtime when I think of Susie. If I had children, I believe that their bodies would betray them.

. ·.

> Both of your parents carry a gene with a mutation, which causes a 25% (1 in 4) risk for each of their off-spring to receive a "double dose" of the mutated gene that causes Kostmann syndrome. Furthermore, this means that you have a 2 in 3 or 67% chance of being a carrier for this condition. . . . At the present time, we have been unable to find information about any available carrier testing.
>
> —Emory University School of Medicine
> Genetics Laboratory, 1999

Mickey and I had been married eleven months when we sat in an overheated medical center conference room and listened to a geneticist—a perky woman with a ponytail—chirp statistics about mutations, defects, and multiple births. While she talked, she turned shiny plastic flip cards that showed pictures of chromosomes. Did we remember studying Mendel and his peas? she asked, gauging our knowledge. Distracted, I heard her say *Mengele's* peas.

The grainy gray pictures on the flash cards looked like magnified images of tapeworms. The chromosomes on the cards belonged to strangers; they were not photographs from my own body. They were stand-ins that couldn't tell me anything.

Mickey knew my fears about having and losing children. By the time we had been together a few months, he knew my sisters, too, from their photographs and my stories. I mentioned Susie and Sarah in conversation often, unintentionally speaking about them in the present tense, as if they were merely absent from the room.

"Sarah makes good spaghetti," I offered one night, dicing fresh tomatoes for pasta.

Sometimes I mixed verb tenses, snaring a sister in temporal limbo. "Susie had the best laugh," I told Mickey. "You would like her." Susie was present and extinct in the same breath.

How long had I done this? I wondered. When, after which death, did this habit arise? When I first caught myself referring to my sisters in the present tense, I felt stupid and a little embarrassed. I knew the truth, so what was I trying to accomplish? Speaking of Susie and Sarah with *is* and *has*, I unconsciously deny what is true of them and true of me. I am sisterless. I had sisters. Were three, now me.

Speaking of them in the present tense contradicts the truth: I am the only one left.

21.

She took some twigs she found in the water and
made a raft with a sail that she let dry. The sail was a
peice [*sic*] of cloth. She sailed on 'till she came to
land.

—From a storybook Susie wrote and illustrated for Sarah,
called "Mrs. Spider and the Giant," circa 1969

Mickey draws me while I sleep. He does this when we
travel: on vacation, or visiting family, another time when an
ice storm knocked our power out and we escaped the freezing darkness at home for a heated motel. He drew a picture
of me on the wall of his study. I am awake in this one, de-
picted as a nearly life-sized cartoon superhero. I have heart-
shaped insignia on my boots and on the clasp that holds my
cape closed.

My husband did not know that when I was little, before
Sarah was born and before Susie got sick, I sometimes

pretended I was a hero who saved people in trouble. This seemed a rewarding way to live, magnanimous and kind, that would earn accolades I would modestly deny. Heroes save because they love. Trouble could be banished, never to return. I lived in a gentle world. As the first child and elder sister, my natural role was favored child and protector of the small. Hercules and Abiyoyo were my first role models. My grandfather and father replaced them, once I learned the stories of their real-life battles for justice. In time, my mother became my hero, although hers was a skill I could not easily emulate. Even in the worst circumstances, she made an effort to love life.

Observing the adults around me when Susie died, I noticed for the first time but not the last that survivors make one of two choices. Either the survivor caves in for the long term, or she decides to keep moving, as if living after the death of a loved one placed her on the kind of moving sidewalk you see in airports and shopping malls. Standing upright and holding the handrails would deliver her, at some future point, back into her life in progress. This is a decision that might not be made consciously. My family's survivors were one day startled to find that we had decided to keep moving.

There was no single moment when I made the choice not to cave in; I just stayed upright and held on. I held on in Los Angeles, warming my skin under the beachy glare. I held on at my mother's house the day of Sarah's funeral, when I confronted my father for leaving me. I held on when I bought the headstone for Susie's grave, and I held on during a summer night in Atlanta, peeling grease-spattered wallpaper printed with smiling teapots from my kitchen walls.

I first noticed that I had arrived at my life in progress when I caught myself talking in that empty kitchen. I lived alone: I was addressing myself. The act of talking to myself wasn't what startled me. What startled me was that I was happy.

There are times when I slip up, when time runs backward and I say without thinking, "I wish I were dead." I say this under my breath when a stack of paper slides off my desk, or I discover that the blouse I want to wear has lost a button, or I can't find a parking space and am running late. The words come in a monotone, triggered by a minor transgression.

When I catch myself saying these words, my heart races (clearly alive), and instinct claps my hands over my mouth. The "it" that eclipsed my family and terrified me when I was ten and eleven years old could still loiter over my shoulder, close enough to hear me.

Be careful what you wish for, my mother warns, without knowing my habit. She laughs when she says this. She is a habitual wisher, on pennies found faceup or facedown, and on loose eyelashes caught with a fingertip. My mother dries the wishbones from chickens, and together we pull the brittle Y shapes apart. Silently, I wish to be fully alive, while my mother wishes for my desires to come true.

In my worst moods, I wonder why I am alive. Illness hid in my sisters' cells, but no disease has emerged from mine. You are alive just to *be* alive, I imagine Sarah saying. Susie, forever eight years old, concurs. You are alive because you are alive.

After Sarah died, I quietly appointed myself the curator of a family archive. At a moment's notice, I could put my hands on boxes of correspondence and photographs that my mother had kept, and a lifetime of my own keepsakes that I hauled from place to place for reasons I could not fully explain. I hoarded journals, yearbooks, and elementary school report cards. I put plastic food wrap around disintegrating copies of Atlanta's hippie newspaper, where ads for coffeehouses like the Twelfth Gate and a store that sold stash bags and peace flags preserved my father's era. I kept an answering machine tape with a message from Sarah. I kept a lumpy, cone-shaped clay figurine the color of dandelions that Susie made in kindergarten. I collected evidence, rescuing our past from oblivion. Each item was proof that our lost civilization had been real.

When I moved into my house, I shoved a heavy wooden cabinet into the too small guest room. The cabinet was poorly made and difficult to use; drawers fell off their tracks and could not be put back straight. The shelves were too narrow for storage. My parents had been given the cabinet as a wedding gift from a friend. When Sarah was a baby, it stood near her changing table. Mom stacked clean white cloth diapers in the drawers and piled safety pins with pink plastic tops on the shelves.

When I adopted the cabinet, the wood still smelled of baby lotion and furniture polish. I stored extra linens in the drawers, and cursed the broken runners whenever I needed a clean towel. After Mickey and I married, we decided to turn the guest room into a home studio. In order to streamline, we got rid of the cabinet. Mickey made sure it was hauled away when I was not home. I wept when I agreed to let the cabinet go. Hardly another death, I thought, but even so.

The memories hardest to live with are not furniture or art projects, but the ones I can't hold in my hands. My sisters loved me, and I loved them. I think of the ferocious, hot grip of Sarah's hug, and the brush of her tan winter coat cold against my skin as she propels me out of Harrisburg's small airport. She is sixteen, and her first driver's license is in her purse.

"Mom sent me to pick you up," Sarah says, bouncing on the balls of her feet. "She let me take her car."

We are crazy with excitement. I live in California, and she is still at home. We miss each other, but have grown used to the fundamental difference that keeps us apart. We don't know how to tell each other how elated we are to be together.

Or, I remember the weightless feeling that Susie and I got jumping on our parents' bed when we were six and four. I can feel the springs wobble inside the mattress. Susie and I bounce in our stocking feet, building momentum until we are airborne. We reach for the ceiling. Even flying we are too short to touch our fingertips to the flat white over our heads, and gravity pulls us down. We bend our knees to break the fall, but never enough, and we tumble backward, laughing as we roll into rumpled sheets.

· · ·

A few years ago, I woke in the middle of the night to see Sarah silhouetted at the foot of my bed. I wasn't afraid.

I sat up and asked, "What is it?"

I reasoned that if I spoke as if nothing were unusual, nothing would be.

"What *is* it?" I repeated.

The shape shrugged in the same extravagant way that was Sarah's, and then turned and walked out the door. I didn't get out of bed to follow.

I see Susie less.

In high school, my girlfriends and I went through a Ouija board craze. After a few tries at contacting former pets and rock stars dead of overdoses, I went for Susie. This was against my better judgment, but the spirit of the moment won out. Sitting cross-legged on Mary Beth's bedroom floor, I asked the board about my sister. Where was she? Was she okay?

The planchette under my fingers spelled out "loves you."

My friends and I adjourned from the bedroom, shaken. We had stumbled from mere board game into questionable territory.

These might be brief brushes against what some people call "the other side," the place Sarah said she was heading when she coded, the place Susie sensed when she dreamed of an empty rocking chair. These are, more likely, how my longing for my sisters appears and reappears in my life, the same way the tide offers smooth-edged chunks of colored glass and unbroken, whorled shells.

Whole days can pass now when my sisters are not prominent in my thoughts. Most days, though, one or both of my sisters traverses my thoughts for the smallest of reasons. Two little girls, one dark haired and the other blonde, run hand in hand in front of me on the sidewalk, and I have to turn my head. A song comes on the radio that Sarah loved, and I want to call her and shout the chorus into the phone. In a different life, we would sing together before we complained that our favorite songs now play on oldies stations.

Every December, Mickey and I display Christmas and Chanukah cards on the fireplace mantel in our living room. We spend an evening writing ours, and happy as I am to send greetings to people I love, the fact that my sisters and I will exchange no cards hits me like a punch.

Mickey knows that I will get up from the boxes of cards and roll of stamps at the table and walk through our house alone a few times, as if I could escape tears. When I do come back to our table, my eyes are dry, and my pen is still in my hand. I am ready to pick up where I left off.

. ● .

It's midnight in August 1974. I am up late, as usual. I am almost fifteen. My parents are asleep if they are both home, the TV blurting the eleven o'clock news, then Carson, then clicked off. If my father is not home, my mother has been reading in the bedroom she has made neat and tidy, with the radio turned to the classical station. She wipes Nivea cream on her face, one hand to each cheek, then places her book on her nightstand and turns out the light, free to dream. Sarah sleeps in her bedroom across the hall from mine. I am still dressed. I've been reading, lying on my stomach down the length of my bed, listening as the house goes quiet for the night. Now that my family is down, I am up. I have a spiral notebook in my lap and a pen in my hand. A coffee mug that I keep for an ashtray leans against my thigh. In preparation for writing, I have dumped the old cigarette butts into my trash can and lit a fresh cigarette. My radio alarm clock is tuned where it always is, radio station WQXI, "Quicksie in Dixie." Eric Clapton sings, "I Shot the Sheriff."

I reach over and tug the chain on the desk lamp. The sudden yellow beam of light makes me shield my eyes for a second. I have a lot to write tonight.

I do not write about marriage, or the perfect job, or kids. I do not write about what I want to come true when I grow up. I don't know this yet, but I am writing messages and sending them away in bottles that will wash up on a future shore, where I will find them when I am an adult.

"I am so glad for the journals," I wrote. "It's like a memory bank."

My journals affirm that I was there, too. I was there, diligently recording my existence on the page, reminding myself that I mattered. Death is permanent, but I knew without daring to admit it that living while drowning in dread can be temporary.

I knew then that that my family's rough voyage would end. When it did, my compass needle would wobble, then settle, and point in the direction where I would find myself. I had devoted myself to trying to save people I loved, obscuring what I knew: that I loved myself, too. I could not save my sisters, but in my journals, I worked to save myself.

Years before Sarah spoke the words, I knew without being told that I would be the only one left. Who else would I be then, when I became sisterless? I would be the memory keeper, admiring the glinting beauty of my sisters' lives and the promise in what our family had been. As I admired, I taught myself to see me again: the visible sister, with days behind me and days wide open ahead.

Questions and Answers
with Jessica Handler

1. In your family, death was not discussed, although it touched each of you. How did not talking about your younger sister's death help to keep your sense of family intact? How did the silence damage your family?

> A: In a way, my parents' reluctance to discuss death was a product of the era—this was the late 1960s and the early '70s, when family therapy was pretty new. Had we under-gone this loss today, my guess is that a doctor or social worker would recommend that we undergo therapy as a group. Both of my parents were very vigorous in their own ways—they made very sure that Sarah and I were as immersed in our daily lives as possible. I don't think they saw any benefit to looking backward.

2. You describe yourself as fading into the background, in an effort to alleviate your parents' worries as your sisters' illnesses

demanded more time and attention. Did you ever resent your sisters or your parents for overlooking you in their effort to deal with the more immediate demands of illness?

A: If I did, I didn't recognize it as such. Early on I knew that a kid in the hospital was serious business, so if my parents weren't home, their intent was not to ignore me but to be where they were most needed. Children are surprisingly accommodating and intuitive when they love and trust their parents.

3. Your parents told you several months before your younger sister Susie died that she had a terminal illness, but they kept that information from her. How did knowing that your sister would die affect the way that you saw or understood her? Did you believe your parents wholeheartedly, or did you hold out hope for your sister's recovery?

A: I don't remember holding out hope for Susie's recovery, but perhaps I did. I know that I fiercely did not want my sister to die, but I did not fully understand death as final. I did know that Susie was experiencing something I wasn't, and I recognized that the two of us were moving apart in a way we couldn't control.

4. In describing how your parents dealt with your sisters' illnesses, you depict your father as "heart" your mother as "mind." Describe what you mean. How did their respective positions prevent them from seeing eye-to-eye about their family?

A: People experience tragedy—and joy—differently. Some people react more emotionally, and others go more to their heads. I don't think either is the "wrong" way to handle powerful information, it's simply how the person is wired. My father reacted to things with strong emotion, singing expressively when he was moved by something, or entertaining his friends and family with jokes and stories when he was feeling expansive. My mother often tempered her strong reactions through organizational efforts, like lists and plans. In some families, two approaches might create a stronger unit, but in my family, the difference in my parents' outlooks furthered the sense of disparity and made them, and their surviving children, feel more alone than supported.

5. As the "well-sibling," you felt bouts of guilt for living an ordinary life, going to school, nourishing friendships, attending birthday parties, while your sisters were cooped up in hospitals for overnight stays and testing. How did you reconcile that sense of guilt as a healthy adult, when you watched your younger sister Sarah struggle to make it through a normal day? How, if at all, does that guilt still occupy a space in your mind?

A: There are times when remnants of what some people call "survivor guilt" come to the surface. I have benefited from good therapy, and from being a witness to the best parts of my sisters' lives and my determination to move forward in my own.

6. After Sarah's death, when you realized the import of her words, that you would be the "only one left," was any part of you relieved that your sister's suffering was over?

A: As was often true, I was stunned by the clarity of her viewpoint. She had summed up my future—and our mutual history—in a single statement. In a way, I was relieved that on her worst days Sarah no longer had to suffer, but that never canceled out the fact that I miss my sister. Her absence from the world will always be a loss.

7. In writing *Invisible Sisters* you visited your sisters' medical files for the first time. How did reading their medical narrative change the way you understood them?

A: I was immensely moved by reading their medical files; more so than I had expected. Often, I saw "inside" a day or an event that I had forgotten or remembered only from my peripheral perspective, as in "Oh, I remember that doctor." When I say "inside," what I mean is a doctor's professional point of view commenting on what he or she sees during an exam. My sisters' doctors were wonderful people, but in the files, they did what doctors have to do, which is comment on a lab result or a symptom. While I read their words, what I saw in my mind was just Susie or Sarah, my little sisters. I found that I was, once again, proud of my sisters for doing what they had to do, incorporating elements in their lives that were in many ways very difficult.

8. Were you surprised by the emotions that you faced in writing this book? Did new emotions surface? Explain.

A: I was surprised by how much I laughed while I wrote *Invisible Sisters*. Often, as I remembered an interaction with Susie or Sarah, or looked through family pictures, I found that I was laughing over an old joke or something we had done together. I cried a lot, too, especially when I re-read letters and cards from Sarah to me from my high school and college years, in which she caught me up on family news, gossip, and encouraged me in a sisterly way. I could hear her voice speaking aloud as I read, which was bittersweet.

9. What mechanisms helped you write this memoir, as you relived much of the loss and pain again through first-person narrative?

A: Reading my journals from my teenaged, college, and post-college years brought me face to face with younger versions of myself. That girl often reminded me, in first-person, of my earlier interests. I saw how lively a girl I'd been, and it was heartening to realize that about myself. I also revisited some of the physical places where parts of the book occur, such as walking to the elementary school again in my old neighborhood, or driving the route from my childhood home to where the grocery store and drug-store had been and observing my emotions as I experienced the look and feel of these places once again.

10. As someone who has survived the loss of two siblings and risen above the devastating experience of that loss to celebrate their lives, what advice would you offer to others who have survived similar trauma?

A: Enjoy your loved ones for the people they are, even during the times when you might bicker or have a difference of opinion. Experience your lives as fully and normally as you can. After a loved one has gone, don't be afraid to remember them, even though doing so can be painful. Your life goes on, although you are changed, and it's a dishonor to your loved one and the life that you shared if you limit yourself after their passing.

11. You experienced being the odd one out on so many levels—as a member of a northern Jewish family that moved South, as the only well sibling in the midst of gravely ill sisters, as the daughter of someone calling for radical change in the land of complacency and reserve. How did these factors affect your ability to fit into your new surroundings?

A: My family has given me what I hope is a sense of kindness, fairness, and a willingness to effect social change. Growing up knowing that others are not always given the chance they deserve, and seeing as much in my sisters, I find that as an adult I make an effort to change what I can for the better. As a child, I accepted people for who they were, and if I held back because someone looked different or spoke in a way I couldn't immediately understand, I was encouraged by my parents, particularly my father, to put my reticence aside and to offer my help. The lesson was that we are each human and deserve to be treated well. My sisters believed the same. Our parents instilled in us the concept of *tikkun olam*, or repair of the world.

12. You discuss your Judaism as a latent part of your identity growing up, but not a defining quality of your life. Did your relationship to religion change as an adult, after Sarah's death? If so, how?

A: Growing up, my relationship to Judaism was predominantly cultural. As an adult, I find that my spiritual life is diverse; I practice yoga, I meditate, and with my husband, sometimes attend synagogue. On my own, I light yarzheit (memorial) candles for each of my sisters and for my father on the anniversaries of their deaths. I only had a general knowledge of what the candles were for. I simply bought a yarzheit candle at the supermarket one day and have since made a practice of it. This is my Judaism shining through; I feel that I am doing the right and respectful thing on those days.

13. After college, you did your best to get as far from your family as you could, moving to Los Angeles where, in your words, you lived hard enough for three sisters. Expand on what you mean by this.

A: Moving far away from the world I had known allowed me to reinvent myself in a place I had never, ever been before, or even thought much about. I was in my early twenties and eager for new experiences. As I learned my way around, established friendships, and worked in an industry known for glamour, long hours, and a high energy level, I got caught up in the pace and the excitement. I felt vibrant. I worked and played at full force, and I loved what I was doing.

14. After years of estrangement from your father, you reconnected with him as an adult, ultimately forgiving him his absent and sometimes negative role your and your sister's lives, and offering your company during his own bout with cancer. How did

your opinion of your father change or not change over time? As an adult, could you better understand his erratic behavior after Susie's death?

A: As an adult, I often look back at the situation my parents faced and am amazed by their ability to make it through—an ability that offers, in my mind, testament to their devotion to their family and their innate will to survive. I don't think I was able to see that clearly as a teenager and young adult. My father's heart was broken, as any parent's would have been, and he coped differently than my mother did, although her heart, too, was broken. I admired my father greatly, and still do. I try to keep my father's good works alive in the way I conduct my life. My father and I were both working on rebuilding our relationship when his life ended, and I'm thankful that we had the opportunity to begin that process.

BETH LILLY

Jessica Handler's nonfiction has appeared in Brevity.com, *More Magazine*, *Southern Arts Journal*, and *Ars Medica*. An essay derived from *Invisible Sisters* was nominated for a 2008 Pushcart Prize, and her work has received Honorable Mention for the Penelope Niven Creative Nonfiction Prize. A teacher of creative writing, she lives in Atlanta, Georgia.

PublicAffairs is a publishing house founded in 1997. It is a tribute to the standards, values, and flair of three persons who have served as mentors to countless reporters, writers, editors, and book people of all kinds, including me.

I. F. STONE, proprietor of *I. F. Stone's Weekly*, combined a commitment to the First Amendment with entrepreneurial zeal and reporting skill and became one of the great independent journalists in American history. At the age of eighty, Izzy published *The Trial of Socrates*, which was a national bestseller. He wrote the book after he taught himself ancient Greek.

BENJAMIN C. BRADLEE was for nearly thirty years the charismatic editorial leader of *The Washington Post*. It was Ben who gave the *Post* the range and courage to pursue such historic issues as Watergate. He supported his reporters with a tenacity that made them fearless and it is no accident that so many became authors of influential, best-selling books.

ROBERT L. BERNSTEIN, the chief executive of Random House for more than a quarter century, guided one of the nation's premier publishing houses. Bob was personally responsible for many books of political dissent and argument that challenged tyranny around the globe. He is also the founder and longtime chair of Human Rights Watch, one of the most respected human rights organizations in the world.

.   .   .

For fifty years, the banner of Public Affairs Press was carried by its owner Morris B. Schnapper, who published Gandhi, Nasser, Toynbee, Truman, and about 1,500 other authors. In 1983, Schnapper was described by *The Washington Post* as "a redoubtable gadfly." His legacy will endure in the books to come.

Peter Osnos, *Founder and Editor-at-Large*